In Jesus Name,
"I AM"

A Journey of Becoming:

Renew Your Mind, Speak Life, and Walk in Purpose

Unless otherwise notated all scripture quotations are taken

from the King James Version of the Bible.

Copyright © 2025 by Lanesia D Cephus

All rights reserved. No part of this book may be reproduced or used in any manner without written permission of the copyright owner except for the use of quotations in a book review. For more information, address:

info@lanesiacephus.com

First paperback edition June 2025

In Jesus Name, 'I AM', Volume 2

ISBN: 979-8-9901-383-5-3 (paperback)

Volume 2:
"Purpose, Power & Kingdom Assignment"

Focus:

Walking in purpose, spiritual growth, and Kingdom leadership.

Dedication

To the Holy Spirit,

There are no words, no amount of wealth, no earthly measure that could ever match the value of being led by You. With my whole heart and soul, I offer You my deepest, most sacred gratitude.

This second volume of *In Jesus Name, I AM* was born not only from Your divine guidance, but also through the refining fire of rewriting, surrender, and growth. What once seemed finished, You gently unraveled and rebuilt—line by line, word by word—whispering to me that the revision was not failure, but faithfulness.

Holy Spirit, You calmed my doubts, quieted my nerves, and reassured me that every change was ordained. Through this journey, You have taught me that becoming an author is not just about finishing a book—it is about becoming the vessel that can carry the message with power, purity, and clarity.

You've been my counselor, my teacher, my steady breath when I felt unsure. You've ignited revelation, delivered sacred downloads from heaven, and wrapped me in the security of the Father's will. Every truth penned is because You hovered over the pages.

Thank You for never leaving me. Thank You for trusting me with Your whispers. Thank You for making me brave enough to begin again. May this volume reflect the depth of our journey together and ignite identity, healing, and purpose in all who read it.

To You be all the glory.

With eternal reverence and unshakable thanksgiving,

Lanesia

Acknowledgments

This time, I want to keep it close. I want to honor the ones who have truly been with me, the ones who have held me up, stood beside me, and covered me in love and prayer.

To my mother: You are my biggest supporter. Your unwavering belief in me has carried me through so much. Your love is a foundation that I stand on, and I am forever grateful for you. Thank you for always seeing the best in me and for reminding me who I am, even when I forget.

To my husband: I know it has taken great patience to be married to me. I have been caught up in so many projects, yet you never once stood in the way of my devotion to God. You have been patient, steady, and understanding, and I do not take that for granted. Thank you for being my safe place, for loving me through every season, and for standing beside me in this journey.

To our children and grandchildren: We are a beautifully blended family, and I see the hand of God in us. I believe that God is calling us to be a true community—one that is unified, strong, and unwavering in love. Watching God blend us together amazes me, and I know that we are just scratching the surface of what He has planned for us. I got you all, always.

To my intercessory prayer brothers and sisters: It feels good to have people who pray for me, cover me, and even check me when I need it. Thank you for your love, your prayers, and your willingness to stand in the gap. You are more than friends—you are family.

To everyone who has ever lifted me up, supported me, or simply believed in me—I see you, I appreciate you, and I love you. This journey is not mine alone; it is ours. And I wouldn't want to walk it with anyone else.

With love and gratitude,

Lanesia

Volume 2: "Purpose, Power & Kingdom Assignment"

Focus: Walking in purpose, Spiritual growth, and Kingdom leadership

Introduction to Volume 2: Purpose, Power & Kingdom Assignment 10
I AM a Holy Contender 11
I AM a Kingdom Strategist 13
I AM an Anointed Trailblazer 15
I AM a Kingdom Catalyst 17
I AM a Discerning Voice 19
I AM Strategically Wise Like the Ant 21
I AM Filled with Divine Insight 23
I AM an Empowered Voice of Truth 25
I AM Aligned with Heaven's Vision 27
I AM Anchored in Truth 29
I AM a Vessel of God's Unstoppable Power 31
I AM Fearless in Faith, Firm in Purpose 33
I AM a Steward of Excellence, Positioned to Rule through Diligence 35
I AM a Kingdom Distributor 37
I AM Set Apart, Radiant with God's Holiness and Purpose 39
I AM Accepted and Anointed 41
I AM Ascended – Called Higher 43
I AM an Eagle, Elevated by God 45
I AM Sober 47

I AM a Divine Creator, Bearing Fruit 49
I AM Grounded 51
I AM a Vessel of Truth 53
I AM a Carrier of Kingdom Grace 55
I AM a Kingdom Warrior, Trained for Victory 57
I AM Fearfully and Wonderfully Made 59
I AM Chosen, Anointed, and Appointed for Kingdom Purpose 61
I AM a Voice in the Wilderness, Preparing the Way for the
Kingdom 63
I AM Clothed in Kingdom Authority 65
I AM a Beacon of Divine Wisdom and Insight 67
I AM a Kingdom Connector 70
I AM Unbound and Unstoppable 73
I AM Aligned Through Prayer 75
I AM Heaven's Voice on Earth 78
I AM a Kingdom Harbinger of Destiny 81
I AM Purpose-Wrapped in Glory 83
I AM a Reflection of God's Faithful Friendship 85
I AM Endowed with Divine Tenacity 87
I AM Anchored in Expectation – A Carrier of Kingdom Hope 89
I AM Established in Righteous Wealth 91
I AM Born of the Spirit – A Daughter/Son Anchored in Purpose ... 93
I AM Royal by Birthright – A Child of the King, Called to Reign 95
I AM Fortified by God's Hand – A Warrior Surrounded 97
I AM Cloaked in the Shalom of God – Unmoved, Unshaken,
Undisturbed 99
I AM Strength Restrained – A Vessel of Grace 101
I AM a Well-Watered Garden – Flourishing in Every Season 103

I AM Royalty Crowned with Purpose 105

I AM a Flame Carried by the Wind of the Spirit 107

I AM Above Only - Positioned for Dominion, Not Distraction 109

I AM a Kingdom Lion/Lioness - Fierce in Faith 111

I AM a Divine Creative - Formed to Invent 113

I AM Patient with Power - Calm in Delay, Bold in Destiny 115

I AM Kingdom Honorable - Cloaked in Integrity 117

I AM an Anointed Warrior - Chosen, Precise, and Powerful in Purpose 119

I AM a Willing Vessel - Surrendered, Sharpened, and Sent by God 121

I AM a Disciple in Training - Taught by the Spirit 123

I AM Authentically Called - Unapologetically Me, Unshakably His 125

I AM Moved with Compassion - a Heart Aligned with Heaven 127

I AM a Kingdom Initiator - Bold in Faith, Ready for Assignment . 129

I AM True to My Calling 131

I AM Devoted - Sincere in Love, Steadfast in Purpose 133

I AM Spirit-Led - Walking by Faith, Guided by Divine Truth 135

I AM a Divine Worshipper - Forever Engaged 137

I AM Radiantly Positive - A Beacon of Hope 139

I AM that Guy/Gal - Confident in My Calling 141

I AM a Fireball - Ignited by the Spirit, Unstoppable in Purpose 143

I AM Steady and Strong - Unmoved in Faith, Unshaken in Purpose 145

I AM Rejoicing Always - My Joy is My Strength 147

I AM Delivered - Set Free to Set Others Free 149

I AM Clean - Purified by Grace, Positioned for Purpose 151

I AM Renewed – Restored by His Spirit, Empowered for New Beginnings 153
I AM Transformed – Renewed in Spirit 155
I AM Sanctified` 157

Introduction to Volume 2: Purpose, Power & Kingdom Assignment

In Jesus' Name, "I AM"

A Journey of Becoming: Renew Your Mind, Speak Life, and Walk in Purpose

This book is anointed. Not because of my words, but because of the power of God's Word spoken through you. This is more than a book of affirmations—it is an invitation to step into the fullness of your identity in Christ. It is a call to rise, to shake off everything that has held you back, and to declare who you truly are in Him.

In Volume 2, **"Purpose, Power & Kingdom Assignment,"** we will focus on your **spiritual growth** and the divine assignment God has placed on your life. Many believers know they are called, but few fully walk in the power and authority that comes with that calling. This volume will activate your faith and align your words with God's will for your life.

As you declare your "I AM" affirmations, expect to experience a deeper intimacy with the Holy Spirit and a greater awareness of your Kingdom purpose. God is calling you higher—to operate in your divine authority, to move in power, and to advance His Kingdom on Earth.

In the back of this book, you will find space to **create your very own personal "I AM" affirmations.** Be creative, walk by faith, and boldly speak into existence what God has revealed to you about your assignment. **Journal the supernatural transformations and breakthroughs that take place as you step into your Kingdom authority.** Your voice carries power, and God is empowering you to shift atmospheres and bring Heaven to Earth. **Write down the date of your breakthrough and watch God do the miraculous.**

Open your mouth. Speak life. Walk in purpose. Move in power.

In Jesus' Name, "I AM." And so are you.

Introduction to Volume 2: Purpose, Power & Kingdom Assignment

In Jesus' Name, "I AM"

A Journey of Becoming: Renew Your Mind, Speak Life, and Walk in Purpose

This book is anointed. Not because of my words, but because of the power of God's Word spoken through you. This is more than a book of affirmations—it is an invitation to step into the fullness of your identity in Christ. It is a call to rise, to shake off everything that has held you back, and to declare who you truly are in Him.

In Volume 2, **"Purpose, Power & Kingdom Assignment,"** we will focus on your **spiritual growth** and the divine assignment God has placed on your life. Many believers know they are called, but few fully walk in the power and authority that comes with that calling. This volume will activate your faith and align your words with God's will for your life.

As you declare your "I AM" affirmations, expect to experience a deeper intimacy with the Holy Spirit and a greater awareness of your Kingdom purpose. God is calling you higher—to operate in your divine authority, to move in power, and to advance His Kingdom on Earth.

In the back of this book, you will find space to **create your very own personal "I AM" affirmations.** Be creative, walk by faith, and boldly speak into existence what God has revealed to you about your assignment. **Journal the supernatural transformations and breakthroughs that take place as you step into your Kingdom authority.** Your voice carries power, and God is empowering you to shift atmospheres and bring Heaven to Earth. **Write down the date of your breakthrough and watch God do the miraculous.**

Open your mouth. Speak life. Walk in purpose. Move in power.

In Jesus' Name, "I AM." And so are you.

I AM Renewed – Restored by His Spirit, Empowered for New Beginnings 153
I AM Transformed – Renewed in Spirit 155
I AM Sanctified` 157

1

I AM a Holy Contender

Scripture:

"Do you not know that in a race all the runners run, but only one gets the prize? Run in such a way as to get the prize. Everyone who competes in the games goes into strict training. They do it to get a crown that will not last, but we do it to get a crown that will last forever. Therefore, I do not run like someone running aimlessly; I do not fight like a boxer beating the air. No, I strike a blow to my body and make it my slave so that after I have preached to others, I myself will not be disqualified for the prize." — **1 Corinthians 9:24-27 (NIV)**

Affirmation & Reflection:

In Jesus' name, I am a holy contender - I rise, I run, and I press forward in the Spirit, contending for the will of God to be fulfilled in my life and in the earth. I am in the race of faith, running with purpose, discipline, and determination. I do not compete for worldly validation, but I strive for the eternal crown, pressing forward in my walk with Christ. My competition is not against others but against every distraction, temptation, and hindrance that tries to pull me away from God's calling.

I train my spirit like an athlete conditions their body—I discipline my thoughts, guard my heart, and stay focused on the prize that is Christ. I am not aimless, I am intentional. I am not passive, I am persistent. I do not give up when the race gets tough, because the strength of the Lord empowers me to endure.

Affirmation Prayer:

Heavenly Father, I thank You for the race set before me. In Jesus' name, I declare that I am a holy contender—not for selfish gain, but for the glory of Your kingdom. I refuse to be distracted or discouraged. I will train my spirit, discipline my body, and run with endurance, keeping my eyes on the eternal prize. Strengthen me when I grow weary, and remind me that the victory is already mine in Christ. I press forward with faith, knowing that You are with me every step of the way. In Jesus' name, Amen.

Reflection Questions:

- What areas of your life require more spiritual discipline?
- Are you running your race with purpose, or are you getting distracted?

Challenge:

This week, evaluate what spiritual training looks like in your life. Are you praying, studying the Word, and staying focused on your calling? Write down one specific action you can take to strengthen your endurance in your walk with Christ.

Encouragement:

You were not created to sit on the sidelines—you were made to run and win! God has given you everything you need to finish strong. Keep your eyes on Jesus, stay disciplined, and never lose sight of the eternal prize!

2

I AM a Kingdom Strategist

Scripture:

"And now let Pharaoh look for a discerning and wise man and put him in charge of the land of Egypt. Let Pharaoh appoint commissioners over the land to take a fifth of the harvest of Egypt during the seven years of abundance. They should collect all the food of these good years that are coming and store up the grain under the authority of Pharaoh, to be kept in the cities for food. This food should be held in reserve for the country, to be used during the seven years of famine that will come upon Egypt, so that the country may not be ruined by the famine." — **Genesis 41:33-36** (NIV)

Affirmation & Reflection:

In Jesus' name, I am a Kingdom Strategist. I affirm that God has given me wisdom, discernment, and strategy to steward my resources well. Just as Joseph was entrusted with the economic survival of Egypt, I too am entrusted with the gifts, talents, and opportunities that God has placed in my hands. I do not operate in fear or lack; I plan ahead with faith and wisdom, knowing that God gives me the ability to prosper for His glory.

I am disciplined in managing what God has given me, whether in finances, opportunities, or leadership. I do not waste my resources but invest wisely, preparing for both times of abundance and times of need. The Holy Spirit is my guide in making business and financial decisions, and I walk in integrity, ensuring that all I do reflects the excellence of Christ. I am not just working for myself, but for the kingdom of God, knowing that my diligence will provide not only for me but for others.

Affirmation Prayer:

Heavenly Father, I thank You for the wisdom and discernment You have placed within me. Just as You guided Joseph, I ask that You lead me in every business decision, financial endeavor, and opportunity. I declare that **I am a Kingdom Strategist**, operating with divine strategy, discipline, and integrity. I will not be wasteful, reckless, or short-sighted, but I will be a good steward of every resource You place in my hands. Open doors of opportunity, give me insight beyond my understanding, and use me to bless others through my work. In Jesus' name, Amen.

Reflection Questions:

- How are you currently managing the resources God has given you?
- Are you preparing for the future with wisdom and faith?

Challenge:

Take time this week to review your finances, career, or business plans. Ask God to give you clarity and direction. Write down three specific steps you can take to be a better steward of what He has entrusted to you.

Encouragement:

God has given you the mind of Christ, which includes wisdom, strategy, and the ability to create and sustain wealth for His glory (Deuteronomy 8:18). Walk confidently in His provision and plan!

3

I AM an Anointed Trailblazer

Scripture:

"Follow my example, as I follow the example of Christ." — **1 Corinthians 11:1 (NIV)**

Affirmation & Reflection:

In Jesus' name, I am an anointed trailblazer. I affirm that my leadership is rooted in Christ and ignited by the power of the Holy Spirit. I do not walk familiar paths—I make new ones through faith, courage, and obedience. Just as Paul urged others to follow him as he followed Christ, I embrace the call to go first, to lead with vision and spiritual authority, and to pave the way for others to encounter God's truth.

I do not shrink back in the face of challenge or resistance. I rise in righteousness, lead with purpose, and stay grounded in integrity. My calling is not for recognition, but to reflect the glory of God and awaken destiny in others. I carry the mantle of a trailblazer—bold, discerning, and surrendered—knowing that the Holy Spirit empowers me to lead with impact and Kingdom influence.

Affirmation Prayer:

Heavenly Father, I thank You for anointing me as a trailblazer in Your Kingdom. I declare that I will not walk in fear, but with holy boldness and unwavering faith. Guide me as I lead with humility, courage, and vision. May my steps always align with Christ, and may my path open doors for others to follow You more deeply. Strengthen my heart, sharpen my discernment, and use me to advance Your kingdom on Earth. In Jesus' name, Amen.

Reflection Questions:

- Are you blazing trails that reflect Christ's example?
- What new path is God calling you to lead others through?

Challenge:

This week, reflect on an area where you are called to go first. Seek God's direction and step out in bold obedience. Lead with purpose and invite someone else to journey with you.

Encouragement:

You are anointed to break ground and lead with purpose. As you follow Christ, He will equip you to lead others into their promised places. You are not just a leader—you are a Kingdom trailblazer!

4

I AM a Kingdom Catalyst

Scripture:

"Then, leaving her water jar, the woman went back to the town and said to the people, 'Come, see a man who told me everything I ever did. Could this be the Messiah?' ... Many of the Samaritans from that town believed in him because of the woman's testimony." — **John 4:28-29, 39 (NIV)**

Affirmation & Reflection:

In Jesus' name, I am a kingdom catalyst. I affirm that my presence, words, and testimony ignite change—not for fame, but for the glory of God. Like the Samaritan woman whose encounter with Jesus shifted an entire town, I carry the power of transformation through my witness. I am not moved by numbers or platforms; I move by the Spirit and operate in divine purpose.

God has positioned me to spark faith, stir hearts, and shift atmospheres. I carry an assignment to speak life, point others to Jesus, and influence souls for the Kingdom. My story—marked by grace—is a tool in God's hands. I am set apart, chosen, and empowered to move others toward truth, healing, and salvation.

Affirmation Prayer:

Father, I thank You for making me a catalyst in Your Kingdom. I surrender my story, my voice, and my life for Your purpose. As You used the Samaritan woman to bring a town to faith, use me to awaken others to Your love and truth. Let my influence break chains, ignite hope, and lead hearts to You. I will not hold back—I move with boldness, compassion, and the fire of Your Spirit. In Jesus' name, Amen.

Reflection Questions:

- Where has God placed you to be a catalyst for change?
- Are you stewarding your story and your voice with Kingdom intentionality?

Challenge:

This week, ask God to show you one person you can ignite with encouragement, truth, or testimony. Be bold—God will use your spark to light someone else's fire.

Encouragement:

You are a Kingdom catalyst—your voice, your presence, and your testimony carry divine power. Don't wait for a stage. Move now, and watch God multiply your impact!

5

I AM a Discerning Voice

Scripture:

"My dear brothers and sisters, take note of this: Everyone should be quick to listen, slow to speak, and slow to become angry." — **James 1:19 (NIV)**

Affirmation & Reflection:

In Jesus' name, I am a discerning voice. I acknowledge that God has given me wisdom, spiritual insight, and the ability to listen deeply and speak intentionally. I do not respond out of haste or emotion, but with grace and clarity, led by the Holy Spirit. My voice is not just heard—it carries purpose, truth, and peace because it is rooted in God's wisdom.

As a discerning voice, I recognize the power of silence, the value of reflection, and the weight of my words. I process before I proclaim, and I hear with the intent to understand. I speak not to impress, but to impact. My thoughts are anchored in God's truth, and my speech is seasoned with love, patience, and divine purpose.

Affirmation Prayer:

Heavenly Father, thank You for making me a discerning voice in this world. Help me to be quick to listen and slow to speak, that I may respond with wisdom and grace. Teach me to reflect Your truth in my conversations, and to bring peace and clarity wherever I go. May my thoughts be Spirit-led, and my words glorify You. In Jesus' name, Amen.

Reflection Questions:

- Do you take time to think before you speak, or do you react quickly?
- How can you develop a habit of listening more and responding with wisdom?

Challenge:

Practice pausing before responding in conversations today. Ask yourself: Is my response wise? Is it Spirit-led? Will it glorify God?

Encouragement:

You are a discerning voice because you listen with purpose and speak with power. Let your words be a reflection of God's wisdom and love!

6

I AM Strategically Wise Like the Ant

Scripture:

"Go to the ant, you sluggard; consider its ways and be wise! It has no commander, no overseer or ruler, yet it stores its provisions in summer and gathers its food at harvest." — **Proverbs 6:6-8 (NIV)**

Affirmation & Reflection:

In Jesus' name, I am strategically wise like the ant. I walk with foresight, diligence, and divine timing. Just as the ant prepares without needing external pressure, I steward my time, energy, and resources with intentionality. I do not wait for crisis to drive me—I move with purpose, anticipating what's ahead by the leading of the Holy Spirit.

Wisdom is more than intellect—it is divine strategy in action. I listen before I speak, I plan before I move, and I act according to the rhythm of the Kingdom. My wisdom is not reactionary; it is Spirit-led and rooted in obedience. As I grow in wisdom, I reflect God's order, discipline, and excellence in everything I do.

Affirmation Prayer:

Father God, thank You for the wisdom You've planted within me. Help me to walk as the ant walks—strategic, prepared, and diligent. Teach me to discern the seasons, to take initiative, and to plan with divine insight. Let my life be a reflection of Your orderly wisdom, and may all that I do bring glory to You. In Jesus' name, Amen.

Reflection Questions:

- Am I actively seeking wisdom from God's Word, or do I rely on my own understanding?
- In what areas of my life do I need to apply wisdom more diligently?

Challenge:

Spend time in Proverbs this week, reading a chapter each day. Take notes on practical wisdom and ask God how to apply it to your life.

Encouragement:

You are wise because God has given you His Spirit to lead and guide you. Walk in wisdom, seek His counsel, and trust that He will order your steps!

7

I AM Filled with Divine Insight

Scripture:

"I am indeed a Jew, born in Tarsus of Cilicia, but brought up in this city at the feet of Gamaliel, taught according to the strictness of our fathers' law, and was zealous toward God as you all are today." — **Acts 22:3 (NKJV)**

Affirmation & Reflection:

In Jesus' name, I am filled with divine insight. I acknowledge that God has given me the ability to learn, grow, and understand His Word and the world around me. Just as Paul was trained under Gamaliel and gained wisdom in the law, I commit to being a lifelong student of truth—both spiritual and practical.

Divine insight is not merely the accumulation of facts but the application of God-breathed wisdom in my daily life. I do not seek understanding for my own pride, but so that I may glorify God and serve others with clarity and discernment. My insight is guided by the Holy Spirit, and I am sensitive to how and when to use it.

The Lord has equipped me to learn from His Word, to gain insight through experience, and to be led by the Spirit into all truth (John 16:13). I do not perish for lack of knowledge (Hosea 4:6), but I thrive because I seek wisdom and understanding from the Lord, knowing that true insight begins with the fear of Him (Proverbs 1:7).

Affirmation Prayer:

Father, I thank You for the mind You have given me. You have called me to be filled with divine insight, to seek wisdom, and to apply it in ways that honor You. Help me to be a good steward of insight, always learning, always growing, and always discerning truth from deception. May I use my understanding to uplift, teach, and glorify You in all that I do. In Jesus' name, Amen.

Reflection Questions:

- Am I actively seeking insight that aligns with God's truth?
- How can I use what I discern to serve others and glorify God?

Challenge:

Dedicate time this week to studying a new area of insight—whether in Scripture, a skill, or personal growth. Ask the Holy Spirit to guide your learning and reveal wisdom that you can apply.

Encouragement:

You are filled with divine insight because God has given you the ability to learn, discern, and apply wisdom. Keep seeking, keep growing, and trust that the Holy Spirit will guide you into all truth!

8

I AM an Empowered Voice of Truth

Scripture:

Isaiah 30:20-22 – "Although the Lord gives you the bread of adversity and the water of affliction, your teachers will be hidden no more; with your own eyes you will see them. Whether you turn to the right or to the left, your ears will hear a voice behind you, saying, 'This is the way; walk in it.' Then you will desecrate your idols overlaid with silver and your images covered with gold; you will throw them away like a menstrual cloth and say to them, 'Away with you!'"

Affirmation & Reflection

In Jesus' name, I am an empowered voice of truth—not by my own wisdom, but by the revelation and instruction of the Holy Spirit. Just as You, Lord, guide Your people with a still, small voice, I am called to lead, instruct, and point others toward truth. Speaking truth is not just about knowledge; it is about transformation. You have equipped me with wisdom, discernment, and a voice that speaks life.

Like the teachers Isaiah prophesied about, I am visible in this season. No longer hidden, I embrace my divine calling to speak, correct, and guide with love and patience. I do not rely on my own understanding, but on the truth of Your Word. Whether speaking, writing, mentoring, or leading, I declare Your truth with humility and authority, knowing that I am only a vessel through which You impart wisdom.

I recognize that my voice is sacred. The words I share must align with Your will. I refuse to allow my own opinions or personal biases to overshadow Your truth. I am not just a dispenser of information; I am a guide leading others closer to You. As I speak, I also listen—to Your voice, to the needs of others, and to the lessons You are still teaching me.

Affirmation Prayer:

Father, I thank You for calling me to be an empowered voice of truth. Let my words be filled with wisdom and grace. Let my message lead others to righteousness and deeper intimacy with You. Remove any pride, impatience, or distraction that would hinder me from speaking with a pure heart. As I lead, let me always follow Your voice. As I instruct, let me always learn from You. May those who hear me be led into truth, and may my words always bring You glory. In Jesus' name, Amen.

Reflection Questions:

- Am I being intentional about speaking truth, or am I allowing distractions to dilute my message?
- Do my words and actions align with what I declare?
- How can I be more sensitive to the Holy Spirit's guidance in my voice and message?

Challenge:

This week, identify one area in which God is calling you to be a voice of truth—whether through sharing your testimony, leading a Bible study, mentoring someone, or simply speaking life into someone who needs guidance. Pray for wisdom, then step forward in faith.

Encouragement:

You are an empowered voice of truth, chosen by God to declare, guide, and build up His people. Walk boldly in your assignment, knowing that He has equipped you for this divine purpose!

9

I AM Aligned with Heaven's Vision

Scripture:

Habakkuk 2:2 - "Then the Lord replied: 'Write down the revelation and make it plain on tablets so that a herald may run with it.'"

Affirmation & Reflection

In Jesus' name, I am aligned with heaven's vision. My thoughts, my vision, and my purpose are synchronized with God's divine plan. I am not clouded by confusion, fear, or distraction. The Lord has given me revelation, and I receive it with a ready spirit and a sound mind. I don't walk aimlessly—I move with direction, because heaven has already ordered my steps.

Just as Habakkuk was instructed to write the vision plainly so that others could understand and run with it, I am positioned to live with clarity and intention. I embrace God's strategy for my life. I reject double-mindedness and embrace divine focus. I express my ideas, my faith, and my mission with confidence, knowing I am speaking from a place of spiritual alignment.

When the enemy attempts to distort my perspective, I silence every lie with the truth of God's Word. I am not driven by emotion or outside voices—I am led by revelation. The Holy Spirit sharpens my discernment and directs my insight. I hear heaven, and I obey. I see through a kingdom lens, and I act in boldness. My life reflects a clear and purposeful walk with the King.

Affirmation Prayer:

Father, I thank You that I am aligned with Your vision. I reject confusion and embrace kingdom clarity. Thank You for divine strategies, clear direction, and purpose-driven plans. As I write the vision You have given me, help me to make it plain—not only for myself but for those You've called me to lead and impact. Let Your wisdom guide every step. In Jesus' name, Amen.

Reflection Questions:

- Am I seeking God for clarity before making decisions?
- Do I allow fear or doubt to cloud my vision?
- How can I ensure that my words and actions are clear and purposeful?

Challenge:

This week, take time to write down a vision that God has placed in your heart. Make it plain—define your goal, the steps you need to take, and commit it to prayer. Ask God to remove any distractions or confusion, and trust Him to bring it to fulfillment.

Encouragement:

God is not the author of confusion, but of peace (1 Corinthians 14:33). As you seek Him, trust that He will make your path clear and your purpose undeniable. Walk in confidence, knowing that you are led by the One who sees all things clearly!

10

I AM Anchored in Truth

Scripture:

2 Timothy 1:7 - "For God hath not given us the spirit of fear; but of power, and of love, and of a sound mind."

Affirmation & Reflection

In Jesus' name, I am anchored in truth. My mind is strong, my spirit is steady, and my heart is secured in the unshakable foundation of God's Word. Fear cannot uproot me because the Lord has given me power, love, and a sound mind. I do not drift in uncertainty—I am grounded in divine wisdom and led by eternal truth.

Though the world may tremble, I remain steadfast. My thoughts are fixed on what is pure, noble, and eternal. I am not swayed by opinions, chaos, or deception, for I dwell in the truth that sets me free. The Holy Spirit guards my mind and fortifies my understanding, giving me discernment in every decision.

When the enemy speaks confusion, I answer with clarity. When fear tries to rise, I silence it with faith. I am not led by emotion or worldly patterns—I am led by truth, power, and love. My identity is rooted in Christ, and I stand tall, unmovable, and unafraid. I am anchored in truth, and in that truth, I thrive.

Affirmation Prayer:

Father, thank You for anchoring my heart and mind in Your eternal truth. I reject fear, instability, and lies. I receive the gift of power, love, and a sound mind. May Your Word be the foundation of every thought I think and every step I take. Keep me steady in faith and clear in purpose. In Jesus' name, Amen.

Reflection Questions:

- In what areas of my life do I need to be more grounded in God's truth?
- Am I allowing outside voices to influence my peace or clarity?
- How can I deepen my roots in God's Word each day?

Challenge:

This week, find three scriptures that speak to truth and stability. Write them down, memorize them, and declare them over your life every morning. Let God's Word be your anchor in every decision and challenge.

Encouragement:

You are not tossed by the winds of fear or confusion. You are rooted in the Word, built on the Rock, and upheld by grace. Stand tall, beloved—you are anchored in truth, and the truth makes you free (John 8:32)!

11

I AM a Vessel of God's Unstoppable Power

Scripture:

Luke 24:49 - "And, behold, I send the promise of my Father upon you: but tarry ye in the city of Jerusalem, until ye be endued with power from on high."

Affirmation & Reflection

In Jesus' name, I am a vessel of God's unstoppable power. Not by my own strength, but by the power of the Holy Spirit who dwells within me. The same Spirit that fell on the disciples in the Upper Room is alive in me today. I am not weak, I am not defeated—I am filled with divine power from on high, equipped to do the will of my Father.

When I feel weary, I remember that the power of God is not based on my emotions or circumstances. His power is a gift, promised to me through Christ. I walk in that power, speaking with boldness, moving in authority, and declaring victory over every challenge in my life.

I do not shrink back in fear; I step forward in faith. I do not walk in uncertainty; I stand firm in the Word of God. The power within me is not just for my own benefit—it is for Kingdom work. My words, my actions, and my prayers carry weight because they are backed by the Spirit of God. I am a vessel of His power, and I will use it to bring light into dark places, healing to the broken, and truth to those who are lost.

Affirmation Prayer:

Father, I thank You for the power You have placed within me. I receive the promise of the Holy Spirit and walk in the authority given to me through Christ. I will not live in weakness or doubt, but in the fullness of Your strength. Let Your power flow through me, guiding my steps and fueling my purpose. In Jesus' name, Amen.

Reflection Questions:

- Do I truly believe that I have been given power through the Holy Spirit?
- In what areas of my life do I need to walk in more spiritual authority?
- How can I use the power God has given me to glorify Him and serve others?

Challenge:

Each morning, declare: "I have received power from on high. I walk in authority, I move in faith, and I live in victory." When faced with opposition, remind yourself that you are not powerless—you are filled with divine strength to overcome.

Encouragement:

God's power is not reserved for a select few—it is promised to all who believe in Him. You are not ordinary; you are anointed, empowered, and chosen. Stand tall, walk boldly, and operate in the power that has been given to you through Jesus Christ!

12

I AM Fearless in Faith, Firm in Purpose

Scripture:

Numbers 13:30 - "And Caleb stilled the people before Moses, and said, Let us go up at once, and possess it; for we are well able to overcome it."

Affirmation & Reflection

In Jesus' name, I am fearless in faith, firm in purpose! Just as Caleb stood in boldness, trusting in Your promise, Lord, I refuse to shrink back in fear. When others see obstacles, I see opportunities for Your power to be revealed. When doubt tries to creep in, I stand firm on Your Word, knowing that I am well able to overcome anything that stands in my way.

Father, You did not call me to be timid or hesitant. You have given me a spirit of faith and determination. I silence every voice of fear, discouragement, and doubt. I choose to speak life and truth, declaring that I am more than a conqueror through Christ Jesus. I am not controlled by what I see, but by what You have spoken. If You have called me to it, You have already equipped me for it.

Just like Caleb, I am ready to move forward in confidence. No giant is too big, no wall is too high, and no battle is too hard when You are with me. My courage is not my own—it is a divine boldness given by the Great I AM!

Affirmation Prayer:

Heavenly Father, I thank You for filling me with courage. I will not fear, I will not waver, and I will not retreat. Strengthen my heart to trust in Your promises, just as Caleb did. Let my faith be bigger than my fear, and may my confidence always rest in You. I walk forward boldly, knowing that You go before me. In Jesus' name, Amen.

Reflection Questions:

- Am I allowing fear to stop me from stepping into God's promises?
- How can I develop a mindset like Caleb, seeing victory instead of defeat?
- What situation in my life requires me to be courageous today?

Challenge:

Every time fear tries to hold you back, declare: "I am fearless in faith, firm in purpose. God has equipped me. I will go forward in faith!" Stand firm in His promises and walk boldly into your calling!

Encouragement:

You are not alone in your battles—God is with you! Just as Caleb believed, trust that you are well able to overcome. Walk in courage, knowing that nothing can stand against the power of the Great I AM!

13

I AM a Steward of Excellence, Positioned to Rule through Diligence

Scripture:

Proverbs 12:24 – "The hand of the diligent shall bear rule: but the slothful shall be under tribute."

Affirmation & Reflection:

In Jesus' name, I am a steward of excellence, positioned to rule through diligence. God has entrusted me with purpose, gifts, time, and influence—not to waste, but to work with intentionality. My diligence is not for status or applause, but for stewardship of the Kingdom assignments placed in my hands.

I choose to rise above procrastination, weariness, and distraction. The diligent hand leads to authority, not because of striving, but because of consistency and faithfulness. I do not chase elevation—I walk in alignment. When I show up with excellence, heaven backs my efforts, and God opens doors I could never force open on my own.

My daily obedience, my quiet yes, and my unwavering discipline are all acts of worship. I lead by serving, and I serve with purpose. Whether it's ministry, business, family, or personal growth, I understand that every area of my life is sacred when surrendered to God. I am diligent, and because of that, I will rule.

Affirmation Prayer:

Father, thank You for making me a steward of excellence. Strengthen my hands to work with purpose and my heart to serve with joy. Keep me focused, faithful, and fruitful. Let my diligence honor You and position me for divine promotion. I will not waste what You've placed in my care—I will build, sow, lead, and finish well. In Jesus' name, Amen.

Reflection Questions:

- Where is God calling me to elevate my diligence and discipline?
- How am I managing what I've been given—am I stewarding it with excellence?
- What mindset shifts do I need to embrace to lead and serve more effectively?

Challenge:

Choose one area in your life this week that needs renewed focus. Commit to working in that area with excellence for the next 7 days. Declare daily: *"I am a steward of excellence, positioned to rule through diligence."* Watch how consistency activates progress.

Encouragement:

Diligence may feel ordinary—but it's producing extraordinary results in the Spirit. Stay the course. Your excellence is noticed in heaven and will be rewarded on earth. Don't just work hard—work unto the Lord. You are not just surviving... you are ruling through diligence.

14

I AM a Kingdom Distributor

Scripture:

Matthew 2:11 - *"And when they were come into the house, they saw the young child with Mary his mother, and fell down, and worshipped him: and when they had opened their treasures, they presented unto him gifts; gold, and frankincense, and myrrh."*

Affirmation & Reflection

In Jesus' name, I am a Kingdom distributor, sowing with purpose and reaping with joy. Like the wise men, I offer what I have as worship—intentionally, sacrificially, and reverently. My giving is not random or ritualistic—it is prophetic, aligned with Heaven's agenda.

God has entrusted me with gifts, resources, time, and influence—not for hoarding, but for releasing at the appointed time and in the appointed places. I give not to be seen, but to honor the King. I don't give grudgingly or out of obligation, but with joy, knowing I am participating in something eternal.

When I sow, I shift atmospheres. When I release, I release blessing. My generosity is a key that opens doors—not only for others, but for my own life. I am not just a giver—I am a steward of divine assignments, and every seed I sow is marked with purpose. I trust the God of the harvest to bring forth fruit in due season.

Affirmation Prayer

Father, thank You for making me a vessel of generosity. I surrender what's in my hands, knowing it came from You. Teach me to give as an act of worship, to sow with divine intention, and to release what I've been given without fear. May every gift I offer be like the wise men's—sacred, strategic, and full of meaning. Use me as a Kingdom distributor to meet needs, advance Your work, and glorify Your name. In Jesus' name, Amen.

Reflection Questions

- Am I giving out of routine, or am I sowing with Kingdom purpose?
- What has God placed in my hands that He's asking me to release?
- How can my giving become an act of worship and leadership?

Challenge

This week, identify one way you can intentionally sow into someone's life—whether it's time, a gift, encouragement, or a financial seed. Pray before you give, asking the Holy Spirit to guide the when, how, and to whom. Then release it with joy, trusting that God will multiply the impact.

Encouragement

You are not just a giver—you are a Kingdom distributor. Your seed may leave your hand, but it never leaves your life. It enters your future, multiplied by grace, favor, and eternal purpose. Keep sowing. Keep trusting. Your giving is shifting lives and honoring the King.

15

I AM Set Apart, Radiant with God's Holiness and Purpose

Scripture:

2 Peter 3:11 - *"Seeing then that all these things shall be dissolved, what manner of persons ought ye to be in all holy conversation and godliness?"*

Affirmation & Reflection

In Jesus' name, I am set apart—radiant with God's holiness and purpose! Lord, in a world that is passing away, You have called me to live with eternal vision. I embrace the high calling of holiness, not as a burden, but as a beautiful reflection of who You are within me. I am not my own—I have been marked, chosen, and consecrated for Kingdom assignment.

Holiness is not about perfection—it's about surrender. Daily, I yield to the work of the Holy Spirit, allowing Him to cleanse my heart, renew my mind, and align my life with Your will. I resist compromise and cast off anything that pollutes my purpose. I walk with reverence, not fear; with conviction, not condemnation.

I carry Your presence, and I represent Your Kingdom. I live differently because I've been set apart. My words, decisions, and lifestyle declare that I belong to You. Your light shines through me, and Your purpose guides me. I am holy—not because of who I am, but because of who You are in me.

Affirmation Prayer:

Heavenly Father, thank You for setting me apart for Your glory. I choose to walk in holiness, reflecting Your nature in every area of my life. Let my words be seasoned with grace, my heart be purified by truth, and my purpose be driven by Your Spirit. Help me to live with intention, knowing that You have called me to shine. In Jesus' name, Amen.

Reflection Questions:

- In what areas of my life am I called to walk in greater purity and purpose?
- How can I surrender more fully to the Holy Spirit's refining work?
- What does it look like for me to live as one who is "set apart" in my daily environment?

Challenge:

This week, evaluate your lifestyle through the lens of holiness. Are your thoughts, habits, and conversations aligning with God's character? Declare daily: *"I am holy. I am set apart, radiant with God's purpose. I reflect His glory and walk in His righteousness."*

Encouragement:

You don't walk this journey alone. Holiness is a work of grace and a partnership with the Spirit of God. As you draw near to Him, He will shape you into a vessel of honor. Stay surrendered, stay radiant—your life is a living testimony of His holiness!

16

I AM Accepted and Anointed

Scripture:

Ephesians 1:6 – "To the praise of the glory of His grace, wherein He hath made us accepted in the beloved."

Affirmation & Reflection

In Jesus' name, I am accepted and anointed! I am not merely tolerated—I am *approved, affirmed,* and *appointed* by the Most High. Through Christ, I am welcomed into divine fellowship and wrapped in the garments of grace. I am no longer searching for belonging—I *belong* to the One who created me on purpose, for purpose.

Lord, You have made me accepted in the Beloved. That means I don't have to prove my worth or chase the applause of man. I am already seated in heavenly places with Christ, chosen to walk boldly in the assignment You've placed on my life. I am not defined by rejection, but by Your divine endorsement.

I let go of every lie that says I'm not enough. I silence every voice that tries to disqualify me. I declare: I am God's beloved. I am approved. I am anointed. I walk in Kingdom authority, clothed in the righteousness of Christ.

Affirmation Prayer

Heavenly Father, thank You for calling me Your own. Thank You for accepting me through the sacrifice of Jesus Christ and placing Your seal of love upon me. I receive Your approval over my life and walk in the power of that truth. Help me to fully embrace my identity, walk confidently in my Kingdom assignment, and extend the same grace and acceptance to others. In Jesus' name, Amen.

Reflection Questions

- Where in my life am I still seeking acceptance outside of God's truth?
- Do I truly believe that I am chosen and approved by God?
- How can I walk more boldly in my calling, knowing I am anointed?

Challenge

This week, confront the areas where rejection has tried to rule your narrative. Replace them with truth. Declare daily:

"I am accepted in the Beloved. I am God's beloved child—approved, anointed, and appointed for Kingdom purpose."

Write it on your mirror, your journal, or your heart—then walk like it.

Encouragement

You are not a mistake. You were never an afterthought. The Father's love for you is not conditional—it is eternal. Your identity is sealed by heaven, and your steps are ordered by the King. Don't shrink back. You are accepted. You are anointed. You are walking in purpose. In Jesus' name, I AM.

17

I AM Ascended – Called Higher

Scripture: *Isaiah 40:31* – "But they that wait upon the LORD shall renew their strength; they shall mount up with wings as eagles; they shall run, and not be weary; and they shall walk, and not faint."

Affirmation & Reflection

In Jesus' name, I am ascended! I am not bound by the limits of this world—I've been elevated by the grace of God. Just as eagles rise above the storms, I rise above distractions, fear, and discouragement. The Lord has called me to higher ground, to see from His vantage point, and to walk in divine authority.

I am seated with Christ in heavenly places, which means I do not fight for victory—I fight from victory. My life is not grounded in earthly systems, but rooted in Kingdom purpose. I embrace my assignment with strength, clarity, and boldness because I am carried by the Spirit of God.

I refuse to settle for low living or small thinking. I am ascended—I soar, I reign, and I rise continually by the strength of the Lord.

Affirmation Prayer

Heavenly Father, thank You for lifting me above every weight and limitation. I declare that I am ascended in You—my vision is lifted, my purpose is clear, and my authority is real. Help me to live from the seat You've given me in Christ Jesus. Let my decisions reflect heaven's wisdom and my words echo heaven's truth. I rise in grace, I rise in strength, I rise in purpose. In Jesus' name, Amen.

Reflection Questions

- Where in my life have I been living "beneath" what God has already elevated me above?
- What does it mean for me to live from a heavenly perspective, not just an earthly one?
- How can I practically align my actions with my ascended position in Christ?

Challenge

This week, write down 3 areas where God is calling you higher—spiritually, mentally, or in leadership. For each one, declare:

"I am not stuck—I am seated. I am not chasing—I am reigning. I am not beneath—I am ascended in Christ."

Watch how your mindset shifts when you speak from where you've been seated.

Encouragement

Don't forget—you were never meant to stay grounded. You were built to soar. The same Spirit that raised Jesus from the dead dwells in you and lifts you daily. Rise above the noise. Elevation is not coming—it's already yours.

18

I AM an Eagle, Elevated by God

Scripture: Psalm 103:5 – *"Who satisfies your mouth with good things, so that your youth is renewed like the eagle's."*

Affirmation & Reflection:

In Jesus' name, I am an eagle—elevated by God, empowered by His Spirit, and unstoppable in my divine assignment. The Lord renews my strength daily, filling me with fresh power and vision. Like the eagle, I rise above challenges, soaring high above every storm and distraction that tries to weigh me down.

God satisfies my soul with His goodness, and in His presence, I am refreshed and renewed. I am equipped with heavenly insight and divine strength to fulfill the purpose He has placed upon my life. I refuse to be grounded by fear, doubt, or limitation because my God lifts me higher than I could ever ascend on my own.

I am not limited by my past or my circumstances; I am soaring in my calling, moving with clarity, focus, and unstoppable momentum. My wings are spread by the Spirit, and I navigate my kingdom assignment with confidence and grace.

Affirmation Prayer:

Heavenly Father, thank You for renewing my strength and satisfying my soul with Your goodness. Help me to rise daily like the eagle, empowered by Your Spirit to fulfill every divine assignment You have given me. Let me soar above fear, doubt, and every challenge. I declare that I am elevated, unstoppable, and victorious through You. In Jesus' name, Amen.

Reflection Questions:

- In what areas of my life do I need to trust God to renew my strength and lift me higher?
- What storms or challenges am I facing that require me to soar with faith like an eagle?
- How can I cultivate daily dependence on God's Spirit to empower my purpose and kingdom assignment?

Challenge:

This week, commit to renewing your strength through God's Word and prayer. Each day, declare: "I am an eagle, empowered and elevated by God's Spirit. I soar above every obstacle with renewed strength." Take note of how this mindset shifts your perspective and actions.

Encouragement:

Remember, God's strength in you is greater than any challenge before you. When you rely on Him, you are lifted beyond limitations and empowered to accomplish your purpose with clarity and power. Soar boldly in your calling!

19

I AM Sober

Scripture: Titus 2:2 - *"That the aged men be sober, grave, temperate, sound in faith, in charity, in patience."*

Titus 2:4 - *"That they may teach the young women to be sober, to love their husbands, to love their children."*

Affirmation & Reflection

In Jesus' name, I am sober! Lord, You have called me to a life of self-control, discipline, and sound judgment. I reject confusion, impulsiveness, and anything that clouds my mind or spirit. My thoughts, emotions, and actions are guided by Your wisdom, not by fleeting desires or worldly temptations.

Father, You have given me a sound mind, and I walk in clarity, purpose, and divine order. Sobriety is not just about what I avoid but about what I embrace—Your truth, Your peace, and Your will for my life. I will not be swayed by distractions, but I will remain steadfast in faith, walking in the patience and love You have called me to.

I declare that I am vigilant and aware. My spirit is alert to the leading of the Holy Spirit, and I do not allow anything to dull my spiritual senses. I choose wisdom over impulse, righteousness over recklessness, and peace over chaos. I will be an example to those around me, leading with a sober heart, mind, and spirit, reflecting the character of Christ in all I do.

Affirmation Prayer:

Heavenly Father, thank You for giving me a sound and sober mind. Help me to walk in self-discipline and discernment. Keep me from anything that would hinder my ability to hear and follow You. Let my life be a testimony of wisdom, grace, and temperance so that others may see Your power working in me. In Jesus' name, Amen.

Reflection Questions:

- Are there any distractions or influences in my life that hinder my ability to walk in spiritual sobriety?
- How can I cultivate a mind that is focused, disciplined, and aligned with God's will?
- In what ways can I encourage others to walk in sobriety and sound judgment?

Challenge:

This week, evaluate what you allow into your mind and spirit. Are your thoughts and actions aligned with God's wisdom? Declare daily: *"I am sober. I walk in clarity, self-control, and divine wisdom. My life reflects the discipline and peace of Christ."* Be intentional in making choices that keep your heart and mind pure before God.

Encouragement:

Sobriety is more than abstaining from substances—it is a mindset, a lifestyle of discipline, clarity, and peace in Christ. As you walk in spiritual sobriety, God will sharpen your discernment, strengthen your faith, and use you to be a guiding light for others. Stay alert, stay grounded, and stay connected to Him!

20

I AM a Divine Creator, Bearing Fruit

Scripture: 1 Peter 1:13 – *"Therefore, prepare your minds for action; be self-controlled; set your hope fully on the grace that will be brought to you when Jesus Christ is revealed."*

Affirmation & Reflection

In Jesus' name, I am a divine creator, bearing fruit in every area of my life! God has fashioned me with a unique purpose and empowered me to bring His plans to life. I prepare my heart and mind daily, ready to walk in the grace and power He provides. As I stay focused and self-controlled, I become an active participant in the unfolding of God's kingdom on earth through my creativity and actions.

My creativity is not just about making or doing; it's about cultivating life, purpose, and influence that glorifies God. I trust that my efforts are fruitful because they are rooted in His grace. I am called to be intentional, to sow seeds of blessing and watch them multiply, fulfilling God's divine design in me.

Affirmation Prayer:

Heavenly Father, thank You for creating me with divine purpose and gifting me to bear fruit in every area of my life. Help me to prepare my mind for action and to stay focused on the grace You give. Empower me to walk in self-control and to bring forth Your kingdom through my creativity. May all I do bring glory to Your name. In Jesus' name, Amen.

Reflection Questions:

- How am I preparing my mind and heart to walk in my God-given purpose daily?

- In what ways can I be more intentional about bearing fruit in my life and leadership?

- What distractions or fears do I need to surrender to fully embrace my role as a divine creator?

Challenge:

This week, set aside time each day to intentionally focus on your God-given creativity and purpose. Write down one practical way you can bear fruit—whether it's mentoring, creating, leading, or serving—and take that step in faith. Declare daily: "I am a divine creator, bearing fruit for God's glory."

Encouragement:

Remember, your creativity and purpose are gifts from God. As you prepare your mind and heart for action, He will increase your fruitfulness. Keep trusting in His grace, and watch how He uses your efforts to transform your life and those around you for His kingdom!

21

I AM Grounded

Scripture: Colossians 1:23 – *"If ye continue in the faith grounded and settled, and be not moved away from the hope of the gospel, which ye have heard, and which was preached to every creature which is under heaven; whereof I Paul am made a minister."*

Affirmation & Reflection

In Jesus' name, I am grounded! Lord, my faith is firmly planted in You, and I refuse to be shaken by the storms of life. My hope is anchored in Your gospel, and I stand unwavering in Your truth. No matter what comes my way, I will not be moved—I am rooted in Christ, built upon the solid foundation of Your Word.

Father, when the enemy tries to pull me away with doubt, fear, or distractions, I will remain steadfast. My heart is settled, my mind is at peace, and my spirit is secure in You. The winds of adversity may blow, but they will not uproot me because I am deeply planted in Your presence. I am not tossed by every wave of trouble or led astray by the deceit of this world—I am established in Your righteousness, walking in faith, and trusting in Your perfect plan.

I declare that my foundation is unshakable. The more I meditate on Your Word, the stronger my roots grow. I will continue in the faith, knowing that You are my firm foundation. Nothing and no one can separate me from Your love. I am grounded, I am secure, and I am settled in You!

Affirmation Prayer:

Heavenly Father, thank You for grounding me in Your truth. Strengthen my faith so that I may stand firm against every trial and temptation. Let my roots go deep into Your Word, and may my heart remain steadfast in the hope of the gospel. No storm will shake me, no fear will move me—I am established in Christ. In Jesus' name, Amen.

Reflection Questions:

- Am I fully grounded in my faith, or do I waver when challenges arise?
- What steps can I take to deepen my foundation in God's Word?
- How can I remain steadfast in hope, even when circumstances try to shake me?

Challenge:

This week, take time to evaluate what your faith is rooted in. Are you grounded in God's Word, or have you allowed doubts and distractions to pull you away? Make a commitment to spend intentional time in Scripture, prayer, and worship. Declare daily:

"I am grounded! My faith is strong, my hope is unshakable, and my heart is settled in Christ. Nothing can move me from the truth of God's Word!"

Encouragement:

When you are deeply rooted in God, nothing can uproot you. Stay connected to the source of life, and let Him establish you in faith. No matter what comes, you are secure in Him!

22

I AM a Vessel of Truth

Scripture: 3 John 4 - "I have no greater joy than to hear that my children walk in truth."

Affirmation & Reflection

In Jesus' name, I am a vessel of truth! Lord, I desire to walk in truth, to speak truth, and to live truthfully before You and others. I will not be swayed by deception, compromise, or the lies of the enemy. My words will reflect Your righteousness, and my actions will be a testimony of integrity.

Father, You take joy in those who walk in truth, and I long to bring You joy. Keep my heart pure, my lips honest, and my mind steadfast in Your Word. When the world tempts me to bend the truth for convenience, I will stand firm in integrity. I reject falsehood, hypocrisy, and anything that does not align with Your righteousness.

I declare that my life is a reflection of Christ, who is the Way, the Truth, and the Life. The truth of Your Word is my foundation, and I will not be shaken. My honesty builds trust, my sincerity brings peace, and my faithfulness honors You. I choose to be a vessel of truth not just in words but in my thoughts, my motives, and my actions.

Affirmation Prayer:

Heavenly Father, thank You for being the God of truth. Align my heart with Your truth so that I may walk in integrity every day. Let my words be seasoned with grace and my actions reflect the sincerity of my faith. May I bring You joy as I live a life that honors You in honesty and righteousness. In Jesus' name, Amen.

Reflection Questions:

- Am I walking in truth in every area of my life?
- Are there any areas where I struggle with honesty before God and others?
- How can I grow in integrity and transparency in my daily walk?

Challenge:

This week, examine your conversations, commitments, and actions. Are they rooted in truth? Ask the Holy Spirit to reveal any areas where you need to grow in honesty and integrity. Declare daily:

"I am a vessel of truth! My words, my actions, and my heart reflect the truth of God. I walk in integrity, and I bring joy to my Father by living in His truth."

Encouragement:

Truth is not just something you speak—it's something you live. As you walk in truth, you reflect the very nature of God. Stay rooted in His Word, and let His truth guide your every step!

23

I AM a Carrier of Kingdom Grace

Scripture:

John 8:10-11 – *"When Jesus had lifted up Himself, and saw none but the woman, He said unto her, 'Woman, where are those thine accusers? Hath no man condemned thee?' She said, 'No man, Lord.' And Jesus said unto her, 'Neither do I condemn thee: go, and sin no more.'"*

Affirmation & Reflection

In Jesus' name, I am a carrier of Kingdom grace! Lord, just as You extended grace to the woman caught in sin, You have entrusted me to carry that same grace into the lives of others. I do not walk in condemnation, for I have been redeemed by Your mercy. I rise with purpose, wrapped in compassion, and assigned to be a vessel of Your restoring love.

Father, I thank You that grace is not just what I receive—it is what I give. Let my life be a reflection of Your gentle authority, Your healing touch, and Your patient heart. I will not be ruled by harshness, pride, or judgment, but I will lead with tenderness, lifting the fallen and strengthening the weary. When others expect condemnation, let me respond with compassion. When the world demands perfection, let me offer grace.

I declare that I walk in divine humility, seasoned with truth and wrapped in mercy. My presence brings comfort, and my words bring healing. I am a witness of Christ's love, and I carry His grace wherever

I go. Grace is the strength of heaven in action. It is the power to restore, to renew, and to revive broken hearts in Jesus' name.

Affirmation Prayer:

Heavenly Father, thank You for Your amazing grace. You did not condemn me but instead gave me new life. Help me to walk in that grace daily, extending it to myself and to others. Let my words be gentle, my heart be compassionate, and my actions reflect the love of Christ. May I always remember that I am saved by grace, and in turn, I will show grace to the world around me. In Jesus' name, Amen.

Reflection Questions:

- Am I walking in the fullness of God's grace, or do I still carry guilt and condemnation?
- Do I extend grace to others as freely as God has extended it to me?
- How can I grow in demonstrating grace in my daily interactions?

Challenge:

This week, be intentional about extending grace to someone who may not deserve it. Speak life instead of criticism. Offer kindness instead of judgment. When faced with frustration, choose grace. Declare daily:

"I am a carrier of Kingdom grace! I am covered by God's grace, and I extend that same grace to others. I choose love over judgment, mercy over condemnation, and compassion over pride."

Encouragement:

God's grace is sufficient for you. You are not bound by your past, and you are not disqualified by your mistakes. Walk in the freedom and power of grace, and let it flow through you to those around you. The same grace that saved you is the grace that will sustain you!

24

I AM a Kingdom Warrior, Trained for Victory

Scripture:

Judges 4:16 – "But Barak pursued the chariots and the army as far as Harosheth Haggoyim, and all Sisera's troops fell by the sword; not a man was left."

Affirmation & Reflection

In Jesus' name, I am a Kingdom Warrior, trained for victory! Lord, You have called me to more than survival—you've called me to dominion. Just as You gave Barak the power to overcome an impossible army, You have equipped me with supernatural strength and strategy to win the battles assigned to my destiny. I do not fear warfare, for I have been forged in faith and trained by the Spirit.

Father, I clothe myself in the full armor of God—not just to defend, but to advance. I raise the shield of faith and declare that every lie of the enemy will fall powerless at my feet. I strike with the sword of the Spirit, wielding Your Word with boldness. My stance is firm in peace, my heart secure in righteousness, and my mind protected by salvation. I am not a victim—I am a vessel of victory.

I declare that spiritual intimidation has no place in my life. Fear will not silence me. Weariness will not break me. I stand as a warrior with Kingdom authority. The Spirit of the Lord lifts up a standard against every adversary, and I will not be moved. I am not just fighting—I am advancing the Kingdom. Victory is in my DNA.

Affirmation Prayer:

Mighty God, thank You for training me in righteousness and preparing me for purpose. You have given me weapons that are mighty through You to pull down strongholds. I will not be passive—I will engage in the battle and walk in boldness. Fill me with divine strategy, sharpen my discernment, and let me move with heavenly precision. Thank You that I do not fight for victory—I fight from victory. In Jesus' name, Amen.

Reflection Questions:

- Am I engaging in Kingdom battles with the authority and strategy God has given me?
- Do I recognize that my spiritual warfare is preparation for greater Kingdom assignments?
- What areas of my life require me to stand firm as a trained warrior?

Challenge:

This week, walk like one who has been trained by Heaven. When faced with spiritual opposition, respond with the Word. Don't shrink—stand tall. Declare daily:

"I am a Kingdom Warrior, trained for victory! I am fearless, focused, and full of faith. I will not retreat—I rise in authority, I conquer through Christ, and I win because the battle is the Lord's!"

Encouragement:

You were never called to fight alone. God fights for you, strengthens you, and goes before you. There is purpose in your warfare and power in your position. Rise up, warrior of God. You've been trained, equipped, and anointed for this very moment.

25

I AM Fearfully and Wonderfully Made

Scripture: Jeremiah 1:5 - *"Before I formed you in the womb I knew you, before you were born I set you apart; I appointed you as a prophet to the nations."*

Affirmation & Reflection

In Jesus' name, I am fearfully and wonderfully made! Lord, before I even took my first breath, You knew me. Before my heartbeat was detected, You had already set me apart for a divine purpose. I am not an accident, a mistake, or insignificant—I am intentionally created by the Almighty God, woven together with care, love, and purpose.

Father, You designed every part of me with precision. My gifts, my personality, my appearance, and my destiny were handcrafted by You. I reject every lie that tells me I am not enough. I silence every voice that tries to diminish my worth. I embrace the truth that I am Your masterpiece, created for good works in Christ Jesus.

You have called me, anointed me, and set me apart. My life is not random—You ordained my steps, and I walk in divine purpose. I refuse to compare myself to others, for I am uniquely crafted by the hands of the Great I AM. I stand in confidence, knowing that I am chosen, loved, and significant in Your kingdom.

Affirmation Prayer:

Heavenly Father, thank You for forming me with intention and purpose. I praise You because I am fearfully and wonderfully made in Your image. When I doubt my worth, remind me that I am Your handiwork, created in Christ Jesus for good works. Strengthen my confidence in who I am in You, and let me walk boldly in the purpose You have set before me. I surrender every insecurity, fear, and doubt at Your feet. I am enough because You are enough in me. In Jesus' name, Amen.

Reflection Questions:

- Do I see myself the way God sees me?
- How can I walk in confidence, knowing I am fearfully and wonderfully made?
- What lies or insecurities do I need to surrender to God today?

Challenge:

This week, speak life over yourself daily. Every morning, look in the mirror and declare:

"I am fearfully and wonderfully made! I am created with purpose! I am God's masterpiece, and I will walk boldly in my calling!"

Encouragement:

You are not ordinary—you are extraordinary in God's eyes. No one else can fulfill the purpose He designed specifically for you. Walk in confidence, knowing you are deeply loved, intentionally created, and divinely set apart. **You are fearfully and wonderfully made!**

26

I AM Chosen, Anointed, and Appointed for Kingdom Purpose

Scripture:

Romans 11:5 - "So too, at the present time there is a remnant chosen by grace."

Affirmation & Reflection

In Jesus' name, I am chosen, anointed, and appointed for Kingdom purpose! Father, before the foundations of the earth, You marked me for a divine assignment. I am not a mistake. I am not forgotten. I am part of the remnant You have called by grace for such a time as this.

I embrace the truth that You handpicked me—not by works, not by status, but by Your mercy and love. Your anointing rests upon me to break yokes, to heal the broken, to speak truth, and to lead with righteousness. I am appointed to carry the mantle of Kingdom purpose, and I will not shrink back from the call.

When rejection tries to speak, I silence it with Your acceptance. When insecurity creeps in, I rise up in the confidence of Christ in me. You have given me authority, identity, and destiny. I declare that I walk boldly in my divine assignment, trusting that You go before me and prepare the way.

I do not question my worth, because You have already qualified me. I am not waiting to be approved—I have already been affirmed by the King of kings. I will not let fear, comparison, or past failures hinder my forward motion. I have been chosen, anointed, and appointed for Kingdom impact, and I walk in it with power and purpose.

Affirmation Prayer:

Heavenly Father, thank You for choosing me, anointing me, and appointing me for Your Kingdom purpose. I humbly accept the call and commit to walking in obedience, boldness, and faith. Fill me with wisdom and discernment. Strengthen me in every weak place. Remind me daily that Your grace is enough, and Your purpose for my life will prevail. I surrender my plans and align with Yours. I declare that my steps are ordered, my hands are blessed, and my voice will speak life. In Jesus' name, Amen.

Reflection Questions:

- Am I living like someone who has been chosen, anointed, and appointed by God?
- What distractions or doubts do I need to surrender in order to fully walk in my purpose?
- How can I align my daily actions with the Kingdom assignment God has given me?

Challenge:

This week, walk with intention. Begin each day declaring:

"I am chosen, anointed, and appointed for Kingdom purpose! I am not average—I am marked by Heaven for divine impact."

Write down what God is calling you to do in this season, and take one bold step forward in obedience.

Encouragement:

You are not overlooked. You are not unqualified. You are not too late. God's hand is on your life, and your purpose is greater than your past. You are chosen, anointed, and appointed—walk boldly in the power of that truth!

27

I AM a Voice in the Wilderness, Preparing the Way for the Kingdom

Scripture:

Romans 8:28-30 – *"And we know that in all things God works for the good of those who love him, who have been called according to his purpose. For those God foreknew he also predestined to be conformed to the image of his Son, that he might be the firstborn among many brothers and sisters. And those he predestined, he also called; those he called, he also justified; those he justified, he also glorified."*

Affirmation & Reflection

In Jesus' name, I am a voice in the wilderness, preparing the way for the Kingdom! Lord, You have entrusted me with a divine assignment—to be a forerunner, to speak truth, and to make ready the hearts of people for Your glory. I am not wandering without purpose; I have been set apart to declare Your will, to light the path for others, and to call forth transformation.

Father, I embrace the sacred responsibility You've placed on my life. Like John the Baptist, I may not always be understood, but I will not be silent. I will speak boldly, lead faithfully, and live righteously, because I know I am chosen and called for this hour. Your purpose for me was established before time began, and I will walk in it with courage and humility.

When weariness comes, I will remember that You have already justified and glorified me. When opposition rises, I will not retreat—I will lift my voice and proclaim Your truth. I was born to point people to Jesus, to stir up revival, and to prepare hearts for Your Kingdom. My call is clear, and my faith is strong.

I am a Kingdom messenger. I will not shrink back in fear, for You have given me power, authority, and grace for this assignment. I am a voice—not an echo—and I will fulfill my purpose with holy boldness.

Affirmation Prayer:

Heavenly Father, thank You for calling me to be a voice in this generation. Help me to walk in my assignment with clarity, conviction, and compassion. When I grow weary or misunderstood, remind me that You have already equipped me to prepare the way. Let my words and life always point back to You. Use me, Lord, to make ready the hearts of Your people. In Jesus' name, Amen.

Reflection Questions:

- Am I boldly walking in my assignment, or holding back out of fear or doubt?
- How can I prepare the way for others to experience the Kingdom of God today?
- What does it mean to be a voice in the wilderness in this season of my life?

Challenge:

Each morning, declare: "I am a voice in the wilderness. I have been called to prepare the way for the Kingdom of God. I will speak boldly, love deeply, and serve faithfully." Write it, speak it, live it—and watch Heaven move through your obedience.

Encouragement:

You are not an echo. You are a voice—called by God, anointed for impact, and positioned for purpose. Keep preparing the way, for the King is coming!

28

I AM Clothed in Kingdom Authority

Scripture

Colossians 4:6 – "Let your conversation be always full of grace, seasoned with salt, so that you may know how to answer everyone."

Affirmation & Reflection

In Jesus' name, I am clothed in kingdom authority and made ready for every good work! Lord, You have equipped me with Your divine power and wisdom to walk confidently in every situation. I am prepared and appointed to represent Your kingdom, speaking words that carry Your grace, truth, and life. I stand ready, empowered by Your Spirit, to fulfill every assignment You place before me.

Father, I recognize that without You, I lack the strength and wisdom needed for my daily interactions. But through Christ, I am fully prepared and authorized to act in ways that honor You. I invite Your Holy Spirit to guide my every word and action, making me a vessel of peace, wisdom, and kingdom influence. Even in challenging moments, I trust that You will equip me to respond with grace and purpose.

I reject any hesitation or fear that tells me I am unprepared or unworthy. I am anointed and appointed for kingdom purposes, and by Your grace, I will walk boldly in the authority You have given me. I will use my words and deeds to build up others and advance Your kingdom here on earth.

Affirmation Prayer:

Heavenly Father, thank You for clothing me in Your kingdom authority and making me ready for every good work. Strengthen my faith and wisdom so that I may reflect Your character in all I say and do. Help me to stand firm in my divine calling and walk confidently in the purpose You have set before me. Use me as Your instrument of grace and power. In Jesus' name, Amen.

Reflection Questions:

- How am I walking in the authority and readiness God has given me?
- In what ways can I better prepare myself spiritually for the good works God has planned?
- Am I relying on the Holy Spirit to guide my words and actions in every circumstance?

Challenge:

This week, declare each morning: "I am clothed in kingdom authority, made ready for every good work. My life is a testimony of God's power and grace." Let this truth empower your steps, words, and decisions, and watch how God uses you to make a difference.

Encouragement:

You are not only appropriate—you are empowered, anointed, and prepared by God to fulfill His purposes. Walk boldly in your identity and calling, knowing that you carry the authority of heaven with you wherever you go.

29

I AM a Beacon of Divine Wisdom and Insight

Scripture:

Ephesians 3:18 – "May have power, together with all the Lord's holy people, to grasp how wide and long and high and deep is the love of Christ."

Affirmation & Reflection

In Jesus' name, I am a beacon of divine wisdom and insight, discerning God's truth in every situation! Lord, I thank You for the wisdom and discernment You have given me, enabling me to comprehend Your love, Your plans, and the hearts of those around me. Through Your Holy Spirit, I have access to a depth of understanding that surpasses human knowledge. You have opened my eyes to see the richness of Your grace and the vastness of Your truth, and I am continually growing in my ability to understand, not just with my mind, but with my heart.

Father, I know that true understanding comes only from You. Help me to grasp the fullness of Your love, so that I can walk with compassion and empathy towards others. When I face challenges or situations I don't fully understand, I will trust in Your wisdom to guide me. I know that through You, I can comprehend things that are beyond my natural ability. I will seek to understand others, listen with intention, and respond with wisdom.

I reject confusion, judgment, and impatience, and instead, I embrace Your peace that passes all understanding. I will trust in Your leading and recognize that You are revealing Your plans to me in Your perfect timing. As I continue to grow in understanding, I will reflect the heart of Christ in all that I do. My mind and heart are open to You, and I am ready to receive all the wisdom You desire to pour into me.

Affirmation Prayer:

Heavenly Father, thank You for giving me the ability to understand the vastness of Your love and the depth of Your truth. Help me to grasp Your ways, not just with my intellect but with a heart of compassion and empathy. Guide me by Your Holy Spirit so that I may respond to others with wisdom and understanding. In every situation, I will rely on You for clarity and discernment, knowing that You are faithful to reveal Your will to me. In Jesus' name, Amen.

Reflection Questions:

- Are there areas in my life where I need to seek deeper understanding from God?
- How can I show more empathy and compassion in my interactions with others?
- Am I open to hearing God's voice and understanding His will, even when it's beyond my own comprehension?

Challenge:

This week, intentionally seek to understand others' perspectives before responding. Let go of quick judgments and listen with a heart of compassion. Declare daily: "I am a beacon of divine wisdom and insight, discerning God's truth in every situation." Allow this affirmation to guide your actions and responses throughout the week.

Encouragement:

The Holy Spirit is your teacher and guide, and He is constantly revealing God's wisdom and understanding to you. As you lean on Him, you will grow in your ability to understand others, to hear God's voice, and to walk in the fullness of His love and truth. Trust that He is leading you to a deeper knowledge of His heart and purpose for your life.

30

I AM a Kingdom Connector

Scripture:

Luke 14:23 - "Then the master told his servant, 'Go out to the roads and country lanes and compel them to come in, so that my house will be full.'"

Affirmation & Reflection

In Jesus' name, I am a Kingdom Connector, drawing hearts with divine influence and bold grace! Lord, You have created me for connection and community. I thank You for the opportunity to interact with others, to form relationships that reflect Your love, and to share Your light wherever I go. Just as You called people into Your kingdom, You've called me to build connections, to engage with others in love, and to invite them into the abundance of Your grace.

I am not meant to live in isolation, Lord. I am a part of the body of Christ, and each relationship I form is a divine opportunity to witness Your love. I thank You that You have given me the ability to reach out, to serve, and to build bridges that bring people closer to You. Whether in small circles or larger gatherings, I will be present, actively participating in community and fostering connections that reflect Your heart.

I reject fear, insecurity, and any hindrance that keeps me from engaging with others. I choose to step out of my comfort zone, knowing that every conversation, every moment of fellowship is an opportunity to share Your peace, encouragement, and hope. Just as the servant in Luke 14:23 was sent out to compel others to come in, I am called to invite others into Your love and presence. I will be intentional about creating spaces for connection and cultivating an environment where Your love is felt by all who encounter me.

Father, help me to be bold, welcoming, and loving in all my social interactions. Give me the wisdom to know when to speak and when to listen, and the heart to make people feel valued, seen, and loved. I know that You use relationships to strengthen us, grow us, and bring others into Your kingdom, and I am honored to be a part of that plan. I will embrace my social calling with joy, knowing that You are always with me, leading me in every conversation and interaction.

Affirmation Prayer:

Heavenly Father, thank You for calling me to be a part of Your body and for creating me for connection. Help me to step out with courage and joy, reaching out to others in love and sharing Your truth with those around me. I will be intentional in fostering relationships that reflect Your goodness and invite others into Your presence. In Jesus' name, Amen.

Reflection Questions:

- How can I make space for more meaningful connections with others?
- Are there relationships I need to invest in or new ones I need to initiate?
- How can I share the love of God through my social interactions this week?

Challenge:

This week, make it a point to initiate one conversation or social interaction with the intent to connect, uplift, and encourage. Let the love of Christ shine through you as you engage with others. Declare daily: "I am a Kingdom Connector, drawing hearts with divine influence and bold grace. I am called to build relationships that bring glory to God."

Encouragement:

Remember, Jesus Himself was a master at building relationships, meeting people where they were, and extending an invitation to experience God's love. As you engage with others, you are participating in His mission to bring people into His family. Trust that every social interaction can be a powerful opportunity to reflect the heart of Christ. You are not alone—He is with you in every conversation, every connection, and every relationship you nurture.

31

I AM Unbound and Unstoppable

Scripture:

Galatians 5:1 – *"It is for freedom that Christ has set us free. Stand firm, then, and do not let yourselves be burdened again by a yoke of slavery."*

Affirmation & Reflection

In Jesus' name, I am unbound and unstoppable! Lord, I thank You for the complete freedom You've given me through the finished work of Jesus Christ. I am no longer tied to the past, no longer shackled by fear, shame, or sin. You have broken every chain, and now I move forward—empowered by Your Spirit and fueled by Your grace.

This freedom is not just for me to enjoy; it is for me to walk boldly in my purpose. I declare that I will not be burdened again by anything that once held me down. I reject every lie that says I'm still bound. I release old patterns, toxic cycles, and fear-based mindsets that once gripped my life. In Christ, I am empowered to rise, to lead, and to move in authority.

I am free to grow, to heal, and to thrive. I am free to pursue my kingdom assignment with courage and clarity. You have made me bold, resilient, and unshakable in You. I embrace this new life, and I step confidently into every room, every opportunity, and every calling knowing that I am no longer a prisoner of my past. I am a vessel of Your glory, moving with divine momentum and spiritual boldness.

Lord, I won't retreat, shrink back, or second-guess who You've called me to be. In the power of Your Spirit, I press forward, because whom the Son sets free is truly free indeed. And that freedom makes me unstoppable.

Affirmation Prayer:

Heavenly Father, thank You for setting me free through Jesus Christ. I choose to stand firm in the freedom You've given me and refuse to return to anything that once held me captive. I receive Your grace to live freely and abundantly in every area of my life. I am free from fear, from condemnation, and from any bondage that would seek to entangle me. I embrace the freedom You've provided and walk in it today, tomorrow, and always. In Jesus' name, Amen.

Reflection Questions:

- In what areas of your life do you still feel trapped or burdened?
- How can you begin to stand firm in the freedom Christ has given you?
- Are there any past fears, shame, or negative patterns that need to be released in order to walk fully in your freedom?

Challenge:

This week, intentionally remind yourself each day: "I am unbound and unstoppable. I choose to stand firm in the freedom Christ has given me." Take a moment to identify any areas where you may still feel bound, and declare freedom over those areas in Jesus' name. Walk forward in the peace and liberty He has provided for you.

Encouragement:

The freedom Christ offers is not limited to a single moment in time; it is a daily choice to embrace the truth of His Word and stand in the liberty He has made available to us. Galatians 5:1 encourages us to stand firm, knowing that no force, no past mistake, and no chain can hold us back when we are in Christ. You are free, beloved, and this freedom is yours to walk in fully.

32

I AM Aligned Through Prayer

Scripture:

Matthew 26:41 – "Watch and pray so that you will not fall into temptation. The spirit is willing, but the flesh is weak."

Affirmation & Reflection

In Jesus' name, I am aligned through prayer! Lord, I thank You for the gift of prayer and the privilege of communicating with You at any moment. You have called me to a life of prayer, to be alert in the Spirit and to watch with You over the challenges that arise. I choose today to remain steadfast in prayer, knowing that through prayer, I am connected to Your heart and strengthened by Your power.

Father, I acknowledge that my spirit is willing to seek You, but my flesh is weak. I admit that there are times when distractions, fatigue, or struggles cause me to neglect the sacred time I've been given with You. Yet, I thank You for Your grace and patience with me. You are always near, ready to hear my prayers and guide me in Your perfect will.

Today, I declare that I will be aligned through prayer, even when the flesh is weak. I will pray with faith, believing that You hear me and that You respond. I will watch and pray in the times of temptation, in moments of decision, and in seasons of both peace and difficulty. I will not allow the distractions of this world to steal my connection with You, for I know that prayer is my source of strength, guidance, and peace.

Thank You, God, that You strengthen my spirit through prayer. I receive the Holy Spirit's help in my prayer life, knowing that when I don't know what to pray, He intercedes for me with groans too deep for words (Romans 8:26). I trust that You are leading me into a deeper, more intimate relationship with You through prayer, and I commit to making prayer a priority in my life.

Lord, I pray that I remain watchful and aligned through prayer in every season of my life. Teach me to pray in a way that aligns with Your will and brings You glory. Help me to see prayer not just as a duty, but as a privilege and a necessity. I choose today to be aligned through prayer, standing firm in the assurance that You are listening and that You are always faithful to respond.

Affirmation Prayer:

Heavenly Father, thank You for the gift of prayer and for Your patience with me as I learn to be more disciplined in my prayer life. I choose today to be aligned through prayer, to watch and pray so that I will not fall into temptation. I trust in the power of prayer to strengthen me, guide me, and keep me close to You. Holy Spirit, help me when I am weak, and remind me to pray when I forget. I commit my heart to You today and every day. In Jesus' name, Amen.

Reflection Questions:

- How often do you take time to pray, and what obstacles prevent you from being more consistent in your prayer life?
- What areas of your life do you feel called to pray over more intentionally?
- How can you cultivate a deeper, more disciplined prayer life that aligns with God's will?

Challenge:

This week, set aside intentional time each day to pray. Start small, but be consistent. Watch and pray over the areas in your life where you feel vulnerable or tempted. Be mindful of the power that prayer has to keep you connected to God and strengthen you in moments of weakness.

Encouragement:

Prayer is not just a duty; it is a powerful tool that keeps us connected to the heart of God. Jesus showed us the importance of prayer, especially in times of trial, and He invited us to join Him in this sacred practice. No matter where you are in your prayer journey, God desires for you to draw near to Him, and He promises to meet you there. You are aligned through prayer, and as you commit to a life of prayer, your spirit will grow stronger, your faith will deepen, and your relationship with God will flourish.

33

I AM Heaven's Voice on Earth

Scripture:

"Then Abraham approached Him and said: 'Will you sweep away the righteous with the wicked? What if there are fifty righteous people in the city? Will You really sweep it away and not spare the place for the sake of the fifty righteous people in it? Far be it from You to do such a thing—to kill the righteous with the wicked, treating the righteous and the wicked alike. Far be it from You! Will not the Judge of all the earth do right?' The Lord said, 'If I find fifty righteous people in the city of Sodom, I will spare the whole place for their sake.'" — **Genesis 18:23-26 (NIV)**

Affirmation & Reflections

In Jesus' name, I am Heaven's voice on earth! I stand in the gap for others, just as Abraham did for Sodom. My prayers matter. My voice reaches the throne of God. I carry the burdens of others in prayer, knowing that the Judge of all the earth is merciful and just.

Like Abraham, I will boldly approach God, not in fear, but in faith, believing that He hears me. My intercession can shift situations, change hearts, and bring salvation to those who are lost. I do not take lightly the calling to pray for my family, my community, and my nation. I will persist, knowing that the fervent prayers of the righteous avail much!

When the enemy seeks to destroy, I will cry out. When darkness tries to prevail, I will intercede. God has positioned me as a watchman, and

I will not be silent. Through Jesus Christ, I have access to the Father, and I will use that access to stand in the gap for those in need of His grace, mercy, and deliverance.

Affirmation Prayer

Heavenly Father, thank You for calling me to be Your voice on earth. Just as Abraham pleaded for the righteous, I take my place before You in prayer. I refuse to be passive. I refuse to stand idly by while the enemy attacks my loved ones and my community. Instead, I will stand in faith, knowing that my prayers move mountains.

Lord, give me the heart of one who boldly declares Heaven's will. Help me to pray with compassion, persistence, and courage. Let me not grow weary but stand firm, trusting that You hear me. Use me to bring others before Your throne, to pray for those who cannot pray for themselves, and to declare Your will on earth as it is in heaven.

I declare that my prayers are powerful. I declare that my voice makes a difference. I declare that I will not be silent—I will cry out to You until breakthrough comes. In Jesus' name, Amen!

Reflection Questions

- What burdens has God placed on my heart to pray for?
- How can I grow in boldness and persistence in declaring Heaven's will?
- Who in my life needs me to stand in the gap for them today?

Challenge

Today, set aside time to pray specifically for someone who is struggling. Stand in faith for them, just as Abraham stood before God for Sodom. Write down their name and a scripture to declare over their life. Send them a message letting them know you are praying for them.

Encouragement

Never underestimate the power of your prayers. God hears you. He responds. Your voice is Heaven's voice on earth, and your intercession moves mountains! Keep pressing in, keep believing, and keep standing in the gap. You are Heaven's voice, and Heaven moves when you pray!

34

I AM a Kingdom Harbinger of Destiny

Scripture:

"About this time next year,' Elisha said, 'you will hold a son in your arms.'

'No, my lord!' she objected. 'Please, man of God, don't mislead your servant!'" — **2 Kings 4:16 (NIV)**

Affirmation & Reflections

In Jesus' name, I am a Kingdom Harbinger of Destiny! I don't just speak words—I release divine assignments into the earth. Like Elisha, I align my voice with heaven's blueprint, declaring what God has already established. I am not moved by what I see in the natural, for I walk in spiritual authority.

God has trusted me to speak into the future—to birth destinies and call forth miracles. I carry prophetic vision and release divine timing into lives, families, and generations. I am a messenger of destiny, a vessel through which heaven announces what is to come.

Like the Shunammite woman, some words I carry will challenge others to believe beyond their circumstances. But I will not shrink back. I will declare the word of the Lord boldly and with clarity. My faith unlocks manifestation. My obedience opens doors. I walk in the authority of my calling.

I am not speaking empty affirmations—I am igniting assignments. I am a Kingdom Harbinger of Destiny, and my words are spiritual keys that unlock purpose and usher in God's glory.

Affirmation Prayer

Heavenly Father, thank You for making me a carrier of destiny. Thank You for allowing me to speak Your heart and declare what is to come. I surrender my voice and my vision to You.

Remove any fear or hesitation in declaring Your promises. Help me to trust the anointing You've placed within me. Let my words align with heaven and cause change on earth. Just as Elisha spoke life into what seemed barren, use me to prophesy hope, healing, and breakthrough.

Sharpen my ears to hear Your voice. Sharpen my mouth to declare Your will. Let every word I release bring transformation and glory to Your name. I declare that I am a Kingdom Harbinger of Destiny! Through You, I help birth purpose, and nothing You speak through me will fall to the ground. In Jesus' name, Amen!

Reflection Questions

- Have I embraced my prophetic authority as a voice of destiny?
- What promises has God spoken that I need to declare over others today?
- How can I boldly release words that shift atmospheres and birth breakthrough?

Challenge

Spend time seeking God about your role in releasing destiny over someone's life. Write down a prophetic declaration, and with prayerful discernment, speak it over them or share it if led. Be bold. Be accurate. Be a vessel.

Encouragement

You don't just speak encouragement—you speak destiny. Heaven backs your voice. Don't hold back! Walk in the boldness of your assignment. You are a Kingdom Harbinger of Destiny, and what you declare by faith will manifest God's plan on the earth.

35

I AM Purpose-Wrapped in Glory

Scripture:

*"And she made a vow, saying, 'Lord Almighty, if you will only look on your servant's misery and remember me, and not forget your servant but give her a son, then I will give him to the Lord for all the days of his life, and no razor will ever be used on his head.'" — **1 Samuel 1:11 (NIV)***

Affirmation & Reflections

In Jesus' name, I am purpose-wrapped in glory! I am set apart, consecrated, and chosen by God. Just as Hannah's son Samuel was dedicated to the Lord from birth, I, too, am wrapped in purpose and destined for God's glory. My life is not ordinary—I carry Heaven's assignment, marked by divine favor and Kingdom significance.

Hannah's bold and heartfelt vow teaches us that surrendering our will to God unlocks supernatural outcomes. I am not forgotten. I am remembered by the Almighty, wrapped in His love, and appointed for a sacred mission. Every part of my journey, even the painful parts, has divine meaning.

God has not overlooked my prayers, my sacrifices, or my tears. He is writing a greater story through me. I live with confidence, knowing that my identity is not random—it's wrapped in eternal purpose and divine promise. I was born for such a time as this.

Affirmation Prayer

Heavenly Father, thank You for wrapping my life in purpose and glory. Just as You remembered Hannah, I know You have not forgotten me. I give You every desire, every delay, and every dream, trusting that You are working all things together for my good and for Your glory.

Lord, I declare that I am purpose-wrapped in glory. You have anointed me for impact, equipped me with power, and called me to walk in bold obedience. May my life reflect Your greatness. May I never forget that I belong to You.

Strengthen my faith as I wait on You. Remind me that in every season, I am held in the palm of Your hand, called to glorify You with my life. In Jesus' name, Amen!

Reflection Questions

- In what ways has God uniquely wrapped my life in purpose?
- Am I fully surrendered to His plan, even when I don't see the full picture?
- What areas of my life can I dedicate more intentionally to God today?

Challenge

Today, offer one area of your life to the Lord with fresh surrender. Whether it's your work, relationships, or vision—dedicate it to Him like Hannah did, believing that God will use it for something greater than you can imagine.

Encouragement

You are not forgotten. You are purpose-wrapped in glory. Heaven has marked you for impact, and God is using your life to display His goodness. Walk boldly. Speak life. Shine with divine purpose.

36

I AM a Reflection of God's Faithful Friendship

Scripture:

1 Samuel 23:16 - *"And Jonathan, Saul's son, arose and went to David in the woods and strengthened his hand in God."*

Affirmation & Reflection

In Jesus' name, I am a reflection of God's faithful friendship! Just as Jonathan encouraged and strengthened David in the Lord, I mirror the heart of the Father in how I love, support, and walk with others. My friendships are not ordinary—they are sacred spaces where God's love flows through me to uplift, restore, and edify.

Father, You have entrusted me to represent Your covenant love in my relationships, and I steward that call with reverence, humility, and grace.

Lord, I renounce every spirit of selfishness, competition, and betrayal. Instead, I choose loyalty, patience, and truth. I will be the kind of friend who lifts burdens, speaks life, and leads others closer to You. My voice will echo encouragement. My presence will carry peace. My heart will demonstrate the friendship of Christ—unshakable and true.

Because I dwell in You, my friendships are rooted in eternal love, not fleeting emotion. I am consistent, dependable, and discerning. I walk beside the broken, celebrate the victories, and intercede for the weary.

I am a living testimony of what it means to be a friend like Jesus—faithful, fearless, and full of love.

I am a reflection of God's faithful friendship because You, O Lord, are the truest friend I have ever known.

Affirmation Prayer:

Father, I thank You for the friendships You have placed in my life. Help me to be a reflection of Your love, grace, and encouragement. Remove any selfishness or pride that hinders me from being the friend You have called me to be. Let my words be seasoned with grace and my actions display the love of Christ. May I always point others to You, the greatest friend of all. In Jesus' name, Amen.

Reflection Questions:

- How can I strengthen my friends in the Lord as Jonathan did for David?
- Are there any friendships that need healing, restoration, or intentional investment?
- How can I be more present, loving, and faithful in my relationships?

Challenge:

This week, reach out to a friend who may need encouragement. Speak life into them, pray for them, and remind them of God's promises. Meditate on 1 Samuel 23:16 and declare daily: "I am a reflection of God's faithful friendship. I am loyal. I am present. I am filled with Christ's love."

Encouragement:

Friendship is a divine gift. Just as God strengthens you, He has called you to strengthen others. Walk in love, knowing that true friendship is a reflection of His heart.

37

I AM Endowed with Divine Tenacity

Scripture:

Luke 18:7-8 – *"And will not God bring about justice for His chosen ones, who cry out to Him day and night? Will He keep putting them off? I tell you, He will see that they get justice, and quickly. However, when the Son of Man comes, will He find faith on the earth?"*

Affirmation & Reflection

In Jesus' name, I am endowed with divine tenacity! I have been equipped by God to stand firm, press forward, and believe boldly. Just as the persistent widow sought justice without relenting, I will continue seeking You, Lord, with fearless faith and unshakable trust. You are the Righteous Judge who hears my cries, and I know that no petition I bring goes unheard.

Father, I reject every spirit of weariness, doubt, and defeat. I choose to walk in Holy Spirit-empowered perseverance. I will not shrink back in the face of delays, resistance, or hardship. I am not fueled by my own will, but by divine tenacity that is birthed in Your presence.

You know the desires I carry and the dreams I entrust to You. I will not stop pursuing You with fervent faith. I am steadfast in prayer, bold in declaration, and anchored in the promises of Your Word. I move forward with spiritual resilience, knowing You reward those who diligently seek You.

I am endowed with divine tenacity because You, O Lord, are faithful. I will not give up, I will not break under pressure, and I will not stop believing in Your perfect will and timing!

Affirmation Prayer:

Father, I thank You for the gift of divine tenacity. When my strength fades, refill me with power from on high. Let every delay build endurance, every test birth greater trust, and every prayer deepen my faith. May my life reflect unwavering perseverance rooted in You. In Jesus' name, Amen.

Reflection Questions:

- In what areas of my life do I need to activate divine tenacity?
- How can I better trust God's timing without becoming discouraged?
- What Kingdom assignment requires me to stand firm and refuse to quit?

Challenge:

This week, meditate on Luke 18:7-8 and declare daily: *"I am endowed with divine tenacity. My faith is strong. I trust in God's perfect timing."* Keep a prayer journal and write down your requests. Stand on God's promises and refuse to give up—He is listening.

Encouragement:

God honors divine tenacity. Your persistent faith is not in vain. Keep praying, keep pressing, and keep trusting—because justice is coming, breakthrough is near, and God's timing is always perfect. Stay the course. You are equipped to endure.

38

I AM Anchored in Expectation – A Carrier of Kingdom Hope

Scripture:

Acts 12:5 – *"So Peter was kept in prison, but the church was earnestly praying to God for him."*

Affirmation & Reflection

In Jesus' name, I am anchored in expectation – a carrier of Kingdom hope! My hope is not passive; it is prophetic. I live with divine anticipation, believing that God will move as He has always moved—faithfully, powerfully, and on time. Just as the church prayed earnestly for Peter, I pray with confident expectation, knowing Heaven hears and responds.

I reject hopelessness, doubt, and despair. I refuse to allow fear to shape my perspective. My hope is not in what I see, but in what God has spoken. I am rooted in His promises and positioned for miracles. I am not shaken by delays or detours, because I trust the God who writes the end from the beginning.

When I feel confined or uncertain, I will remember that prison walls did not stop Peter's release—nor will they stop God's power in my life. I will keep praying, keep believing, and keep declaring that breakthrough is near. I am a carrier of Kingdom hope, called to stand in faith not only for myself, but also for others who need light in the darkness.

I am anchored in expectation because You, O Lord, are faithful. My hope is alive, because You are alive in me!

Affirmation Prayer:

Father, I thank You that my hope is securely anchored in Your Word and Your nature. Teach me to wait with expectation and to pray with conviction. Let my life reflect confident hope, even in the face of uncertainty. Remind me that Your promises are yes and amen. In Jesus' name, Amen.

Reflection Questions:

- Where in my life do I need to shift from passive waiting to active, hopeful expectation?
- How can I become a vessel of hope for someone else this week?
- What miracle or breakthrough am I believing for—and do I truly expect God to move?

Challenge:

This week, meditate on Acts 12:5 and declare daily: *"I am anchored in expectation. I carry Kingdom hope. I believe God is moving on my behalf."* Write down three specific things you're praying for, and approach each one with the expectation that God will answer according to His will and glory.

Encouragement:

Hope is not wishful thinking—it is Kingdom expectation. Stay anchored. Keep believing. What you carry will bless others. What you're praying for is already stirring in Heaven. Breakthrough is coming!

39

I AM Established in Righteous Wealth

Scripture:

Psalm 112:3 - "Wealth and riches are in their houses, and their righteousness endures forever."

Affirmation & Reflection

In Jesus' name, I am established in righteous wealth—a living witness of God's enduring blessing! Lord, You are my source, and every good and perfect gift flows from Your hand. The wealth and abundance in my life are rooted in righteousness, not in striving or self-promotion. Because I revere You and delight in Your commands, You have established my house with lasting blessings, both spiritual and material. My legacy is not only prosperity but righteousness that endures from generation to generation.

Father, I reject the mindset of lack, scarcity, and fear. I am not bound by the world's economy, for I operate under Kingdom provision. I choose to walk by faith and not by sight, knowing that Your blessings overflow in every area of my life—health, wisdom, peace, relationships, and finances. You take pleasure in the prosperity of Your servant, and I walk boldly in that truth.

I declare that I am a good steward of all You've entrusted to me. My resources are tools for Kingdom advancement. I sow generously, I serve joyfully, and I give without hesitation, knowing I live under an open Heaven. I do not chase blessings—they follow me, for Your hand is upon me. I am positioned for overflow and anchored in purpose.

I am established in righteous wealth because You, O Lord, are faithful. My life radiates Your goodness, and I will forever testify of Your enduring provision!

Affirmation Prayer:

Father, thank You for establishing me in Your righteous wealth. Let my life be a mirror of Your generosity and goodness. Teach me to steward the blessings You've given me with humility, purpose, and joy. May I never forget that every resource, opportunity, and increase is a reflection of Your faithfulness. I choose to live as a vessel of Your blessing and a witness to Your glory. In Jesus' name, Amen.

Reflection Questions:

- How do I define wealth in light of God's Word?
- Am I building a legacy of righteousness that will outlast me?
- How can I be more intentional in using my blessings to impact the Kingdom?

Challenge:

This week, meditate on Psalm 112:3 and declare daily: "I am established in righteous wealth. I live as a witness of God's enduring blessing." Journal the ways God has prospered you spiritually and naturally. Then, bless someone else in a tangible way as a reflection of your gratitude.

Encouragement:

You are not called to just survive—you are called to thrive. Your wealth is not fleeting; it is established in righteousness. As you honor the Lord, He will continue to increase you and use you as a channel of His Kingdom abundance. Stand firm—you are a living witness of His faithful provision!

40

I AM Born of the Spirit – A Daughter/Son Anchored in Purpose

Scripture:

Proverbs 23:22-25 – *"Listen to your father, who gave you life, and do not despise your mother when she is old. Buy the truth and do not sell it—wisdom, instruction and insight as well. The father of a righteous child has great joy; a man who fathers a wise son rejoices in him. May your father and mother rejoice; may she who gave you birth be joyful!"*

Affirmation & Reflection

In Jesus' name, I am born of the Spirit—anchored in purpose and called by name. I am not an accident or an afterthought—I am divinely crafted and eternally known by the One who breathed life into me. My Father in Heaven has spoken identity over me, and I walk in the truth that I am His beloved child. My purpose was established before I ever took my first breath, and I live to bring Him joy.

Because I am a daughter/son of the Kingdom, I walk in wisdom, honor, and integrity. I am guided by truth, shaped by righteousness, and led by the Spirit. The legacy of godly instruction has been written in my heart, and I receive it with humility. I choose to live in a way that honors both my earthly and spiritual lineage—bringing joy to those who poured into me and to the Father who delights in my growth.

I reject the spirit of orphanhood and every voice that tells me I don't belong. I am not abandoned, overlooked, or unworthy—I am chosen, cherished, and sealed with a divine purpose. I rise each day with the confidence that I am a vessel of legacy, a carrier of wisdom, and a reflection of my Father's love.

I am born of the Spirit. I am anchored in divine purpose. I am called by name.

Affirmation Prayer:

Father, thank You for calling me Your own. I rejoice that I am not only born of flesh but reborn by Your Spirit. Anchor me daily in my kingdom identity and purpose. May my life be marked by wisdom, honor, and joy—bringing glory to Your name and to those who have guided me. I am forever grateful that You know my name and delight in me. In Jesus' name, Amen.

Reflection Questions:

- Do I live with the awareness that I am called by name and born with purpose?
- How can I bring joy to God through wise and righteous living?
- What legacy of wisdom and faith am I continuing or establishing?

Challenge:

This week, meditate on Proverbs 23:22-25 and declare daily: *"I am born of the Spirit—anchored in purpose and called by name. I bring joy to my Father through righteous living."* Reflect on the mentors, parents, or spiritual leaders who've sown into your life, and honor them with prayer, gratitude, or action.

Encouragement:

You are not just someone's child—you are God's beloved. He takes joy in you, calls you by name, and entrusts you with Kingdom purpose. Walk in that truth. Let your life echo His voice and legacy.

41

I AM Royal by Birthright – A Child of the King, Called to Reign

Scripture:

2 Corinthians 6:18 – "And I will be a Father to you, and you shall be sons and daughters to Me, says the Lord Almighty."

Affirmation & Reflection

In Jesus' name, I am Royal by Birthright – a child of the King, called to reign! You, Lord, are my Father, and I belong to You. I am not an orphan in this world—I have been adopted into divine royalty, chosen by Your love, and secured by Your eternal promise. You have crowned me with identity and inheritance, and nothing can separate me from You.

Father, I thank You for being my source, my shelter, and the King who calls me His own. When the world tries to define me by limitation, failure, or fear, I rise in the truth that I am royalty. My story is rewritten by grace. I am not forgotten or forsaken—I am honored, equipped, and elevated by You.

Because I am Your child, I carry the authority of Your Kingdom. I walk in inheritance, legacy, and purpose. I do not shrink back in insecurity, for I have been called to lead with love and live with boldness. My future is secure because my Father is sovereign.

I reject every false label and embrace the truth that I am Your royal child—marked, named, and chosen. I walk in kingdom confidence, knowing that I have access to Your promises and carry out Your will in the earth.

I am Royal by Birthright. I am a child of the King. I am called. I am crowned. I am chosen.

Affirmation Prayer:

Father, I thank You for calling me into Your royal family. I receive my identity as Your beloved child with joy and authority. Let me live boldly in the calling You've given me, reflecting the values and vision of Your Kingdom. May I never forget that I have been set apart to reign through Christ. In Jesus' name, Amen.

Reflection Questions:

- Do I live with the mindset of royalty or with the mentality of rejection?
- How does knowing I am a child of the King influence my daily decisions?
- In what ways can I walk in purpose and leadership as part of God's royal family?

Challenge:

This week, meditate on 2 Corinthians 6:18 and declare daily:

"I am Royal by Birthright. I am a child of the King, and I walk in purpose and promise."

Write down three ways you can live with Kingdom confidence and serve others with a royal heart.

Encouragement:

You are not forgotten, and you are not ordinary. You are royalty—God's chosen, called to reign with purpose. Walk boldly, lead humbly, and live knowing your place is in the palace of the King.

42

I AM Fortified by God's Hand – A Warrior Surrounded

Scripture: *Psalm 27:2-3* – *"When the wicked advance against me to devour me, it is my enemies and my foes who will stumble and fall. Though an army besiege me, my heart will not fear; though war break out against me, even then I will be confident."*

Affirmation & Reflection

In Jesus' name, I am fortified by God's hand—a warrior surrounded by the Presence of the Most High! Lord, You are my refuge and my shield. When the enemy rises up to devour me, it is he who stumbles and falls, for You have already declared my victory. I am not exposed—I am enclosed by divine fire, protected by Your Word, and kept by Your promise.

Though armies rise against me and war threatens my peace, I will not fear. I stand bold and confident, not because of my own strength, but because I know who fights for me. I am not defenseless—I am divinely reinforced, a daughter/son of destiny with angelic backup and supernatural covering.

I reject every spirit of fear, anxiety, and intimidation. I rise in faith, clothed in courage, and armored in the truth of who You are. No weapon formed against me will prosper. No plan of the enemy will prevail. No darkness can extinguish the light that surrounds me. I am God's warrior, and I fight from victory—not for it.

I am fortified. I am fearless. I am secure in the hands of my God.

Affirmation Prayer:

Father, thank You that I am fortified by Your mighty hand. You are my stronghold and my hiding place. In every battle and in every storm, You surround me with Your presence and power. Let my life reflect the fearless confidence of one who is divinely protected. In Jesus' name, Amen.

Reflection Questions:

- What battles am I currently facing that I need to surrender to God's defense?
- In what ways has God shown me His protection in past seasons?
- How can I respond like a fortified warrior instead of a fearful bystander?

Challenge:

This week, meditate on Psalm 27:2-3 and declare daily: *"I am fortified by God's hand. I am fearless. I am secure."* Each day, write down how you saw God's presence protect or guide you—even in subtle ways.

Encouragement:

You are not exposed—you are encamped by God's glory! Walk tall, speak boldly, and live confidently, knowing the Most High surrounds you like a shield. You are fortified for the fight, and victory is already yours!

43

I AM Cloaked in the Shalom of God – Unmoved, Unshaken, Undisturbed

Scripture: *Matthew 5:9* – *"Blessed are the peacemakers, for they will be called children of God."*

Affirmation & Reflection

In Jesus' name, I am cloaked in the Shalom of God—unmoved, unshaken, and undisturbed. Father, You are Jehovah Shalom, the Lord my peace. Because I am Your child, Your supernatural calm surrounds me and lives within me. I do not merely seek peace—I embody it. I carry Your presence into every room, shifting atmospheres and silencing storms.

Though the world may rage with conflict, my spirit is anchored in divine stillness. I do not panic. I do not react. I respond with wisdom, patience, and authority because I know who I am and whose I am. I am wrapped in the peace that passes understanding, guarded by Your Spirit, and secured in Your love.

I reject every lie that tells me I must live in chaos, stress, or fear. My identity is not tied to turmoil but to Your eternal calm. I am a peacemaker—planted to bring healing, order, and reconciliation in my home, in my circle, and in my calling. Peace is not my weakness—it is my kingdom strength.

Affirmation Prayer:

Father, I thank You that I am hidden in the Shalom of Heaven. Your peace is my covering, my anchor, and my strength. No matter what I face, I will not be shaken, for I am secured in You. Let me be a vessel of Your peace to others. May my presence release calm, and may my words sow unity. In Jesus' name, Amen.

Reflection Questions:

- What areas of your life do you need to surrender for God's peace to fully reign?
- Are you cultivating peace with your words and presence, or unintentionally fueling conflict?
- How can you deepen your trust in God to remain anchored when life becomes overwhelming?

Challenge:

This week, practice becoming *a carrier of peace*. When confronted with tension, pause and declare:

"I am cloaked in the Shalom of God—unmoved, unshaken, undisturbed."

Document every moment where you chose peace over panic and track the spiritual shift it caused around you.

Encouragement:

You are not tossed by the waves—you are anchored in Christ. You are not easily provoked—you are grounded in divine stillness. You are royalty, cloaked in Heaven's peace. Let it rule your heart and overflow into your leadership, relationships, and kingdom assignment. God's peace is not fragile—it is your power.

44

I AM Strength Restrained – A Vessel of Grace

Scripture:

2 Timothy 2:24 - "And the servant of the Lord must not be quarrelsome but must be kind to everyone, able to teach, not resentful."

Affirmation & Reflection

In Jesus' name, I am strength restrained - a vessel of grace and power under control! Father, You are the perfect balance of justice and mercy, strength and gentleness. Because I am made in Your image, I carry the same Spirit that empowers me to lead with meekness, not malice. I don't respond with hostility or pride—I respond with humility, wisdom, and love.

Lord, I accept my assignment to serve with a Spirit-led calmness. I choose not to be reactive or quarrelsome, even when challenged. My power is anchored in self-control and guided by grace. I am equipped to teach, to correct without resentment, and to speak life in every conversation. Gentleness is not my weakness—it is my mantle of maturity.

I reject the lie that gentleness makes me ineffective. I embrace the truth that true kingdom leadership is marked by calm authority, tender firmness, and Christlike compassion. I lead with boldness wrapped in kindness and stand firm in truth without being harsh or abrasive. I am a safe place for others to grow, to learn, and to be restored.

Affirmation Prayer:

Father, thank You for forming in me the gentleness of Christ. I declare that I am strong in the Spirit and clothed in self-control. Help me to lead with humility, to speak with kindness, and to respond with wisdom. Let Your gentleness flow through me as I teach, serve, and influence others for Your glory. In Jesus' name, Amen.

Reflection Questions:

- In what areas of your life do you need to practice more spiritual restraint?
- Are there moments when being "right" matters more to you than being gentle?
- How can your gentleness reflect Christ to someone who is hurting or difficult?

Challenge:

This week, allow the Holy Spirit to guide your responses in every interaction. When tempted to react harshly, pause and declare: "I am strength restrained—I lead with grace and power under control." Track how your gentleness opens doors for deeper connections and greater peace.

Encouragement:

You are not out of control—you are anchored in the Spirit of God. Your gentleness is evidence of your spiritual maturity. Walk in quiet confidence, knowing that heaven backs your soft answers with divine power. Let every word and action reflect the strength of Christ in you. You are a vessel of holy restraint—powerful, poised, and purposed.

45

I AM a Well-Watered Garden – Flourishing in Every Season

Scripture: John 15:5 – *"I am the vine; you are the branches. If you remain in me and I in you, you will bear much fruit; apart from me, you can do nothing."*

Affirmation & Reflection

In Jesus' name, I am a well-watered garden—flourishing in every season, rooted in purpose! Father, I remain in You, and because I am connected to You, I blossom in every area of my life. I do not strive in my own strength, for You are the source of my nourishment and growth. I abide in Your presence, and Your Spirit causes me to bear fruit—love, joy, peace, patience, kindness, goodness, faithfulness, gentleness, and self-control.

Lord, I declare that everything You have planted in me will thrive. My thoughts, my words, and my actions align with Your divine purpose. My life is a visible expression of Your grace, and the work of my hands is fruitful. Even in dry or pruning seasons, I trust Your process, knowing You are preparing me for overflow and greater purpose.

I reject every seed of barrenness, delay, and unfruitfulness. I will not be shaken by temporary setbacks or distracted by comparison, for I am deeply rooted in You. Your Word waters me daily, and in every season, I produce fruit that brings glory to Your name. I overflow with divine abundance, and my fruit shall remain.

Affirmation Prayer:

Father, I thank You for being my Living Water and the Gardener of my soul. I declare that I am fruitful because I am rooted in You. I will not be moved by drought or delay. Instead, I walk in confidence, knowing that You are cultivating something beautiful and eternal in me. Let my life be a garden of grace and a testimony of Your goodness. In Jesus' name, Amen.

Reflection Questions:

- Are you staying connected to Jesus, the true vine, through prayer and His Word?
- What areas of your life need more fruitfulness?
- How can you allow God to prune you so that you can bear even greater fruit?

Challenge:

This week, intentionally cultivate your spiritual garden. Water your soul with the Word, extend kindness, and bear fruit in your actions. Declare daily, *"I am a well-watered garden—flourishing in every season, rooted in purpose!"* Journal how God is producing fruit in and through your life.

Encouragement:

You are not barren. You are not forgotten. You are not stuck. You are a well-watered garden, planted by the hand of God. Stay rooted in Christ, and watch how He brings beauty, purpose, and increase out of every season. It is already yours!

46

I AM Royalty Crowned with Purpose

Scripture: Revelation 1:6 - *"And hath made us kings and priests unto God and his Father; to him be glory and dominion for ever and ever. Amen."*

Affirmation & Reflection

In Jesus' name, I am Royalty Crowned with Purpose – Chosen, Commissioned, and Covered by the King of Glory! Father, You have called me out of darkness and placed a crown of destiny upon my head. I am not a beggar, nor do I walk in defeat—I walk in the royal identity You have given me through Christ. I am a child of the King of kings, and my inheritance is secure in You.

I reign in life through Christ, exercising spiritual authority over fear, doubt, and the enemy's schemes. My words carry weight, for You have placed power in my tongue. I decree and declare Your promises over my life, and I walk with confidence, knowing that I am seated in heavenly places with Christ Jesus.

As Your royal priesthood, I serve with humility and wisdom, leading with love and truth. My life is a reflection of Your kingdom, and I will not lower my standard to fit the world's expectations. I am set apart, chosen, and anointed for such a time as this. I refuse to think small, act small, or live beneath the calling You have placed upon me.

Affirmation Prayer:

Father, I thank You for making me royalty in Your kingdom. I embrace my identity as one crowned with purpose, walking in the authority and grace You have given me. I reject every lie that tells me I am unworthy or insignificant. I reign with Christ, and I live with purpose. Let my life bring You glory as I walk boldly in who You have called me to be. In Jesus' name, Amen.

Reflection Questions:

- Do you see yourself as God sees you—royal, chosen, and powerful in Christ?
- What areas of your life do you need to start walking in authority?
- How can you lead and serve others as part of God's royal priesthood?

Challenge:

This week, declare over yourself daily: "I am royalty crowned with purpose! I walk in authority, wisdom, and grace." Carry yourself with confidence, knowing that you represent God's kingdom. Take intentional steps to speak life into your situations and into the lives of others, leading with the heart of a true servant-king or queen.

Encouragement:

You are not ordinary—you are royalty! You have been chosen, anointed, and positioned by God. Walk in your divine calling with boldness, for you are crowned with purpose and destined to reign for His glory!

47

I AM a Flame Carried by the Wind of the Spirit

Scripture:

Jude 20 - *"But ye, beloved, building up yourselves on your most holy faith, praying in the Holy Ghost."*

Affirmation & Reflection

In Jesus' name, I am a flame carried by the wind of the Spirit—moved only by God's voice! Father, thank You for igniting my heart with divine fire and positioning me to be led by Your Spirit. I do not move aimlessly or react emotionally—I respond to the breath of Heaven. Your voice is the compass of my soul, and in every season, I am guided by Your whisper.

When confusion rises like a storm, I stay still and pray in the Spirit, building myself up in my most holy faith. I silence the noise around me and within me to discern the direction of Your wind. I reject the pressure to be moved by opinions, feelings, or fear. I am tethered to truth, stirred by Your Word, and propelled by Your power.

I embrace the discipline of listening before moving. I walk in divine timing, not driven by impulse but anchored in intimacy. Even when I don't know what to say or do, Your Spirit intercedes through me, aligning my desires with Heaven's agenda. I am led, not lost. I am moved, not misled. I am aflame, not consumed.

Affirmation Prayer:

Holy Spirit, I yield to Your leading. Be the wind beneath my flame and the voice that guides every step. Teach me to move with precision and boldness. Let Your fire purify my motives and Your breath carry me into divine appointments. I commit my heart, mind, and spirit to You—let my life burn brightly for Your glory. In Jesus' name, Amen.

Reflection Questions:

- Am I slowing down enough to hear the Spirit's whisper?
- In what ways do I need to let go of emotional reactions and be moved by God's voice instead?
- How can I deepen my time of prayer to build spiritual sensitivity?

Challenge:

This week, set aside intentional time each day to pray in the Holy Spirit. Journal what you sense the Spirit is saying and declare, "I am a flame carried by the wind of the Spirit—moved only by God's voice." Let this be your posture in conversations, decisions, and spiritual leadership.

Encouragement:

You are not directionless. You are not powerless. You are a child of God, ignited by the Holy Spirit and carried by His breath. Trust His rhythm. Follow His promptings. You are Spirit-led—and your path is ablaze with purpose!

48

I AM Above Only – Positioned for Dominion, Not Distraction

Scripture:

Deuteronomy 28:13 - *"And the Lord shall make thee the head, and not the tail; and thou shalt be above only, and thou shalt not be beneath; if that thou hearken unto the commandments of the Lord thy God, which I command thee this day, to observe and to do them."*

Affirmation & Reflection

In Jesus' name, I am above only – positioned for dominion, not distraction! Father, I thank You for elevating me to walk in victory, not defeat. You have crowned me with purpose, and as I obey Your word, I am established in authority. I do not waver beneath the pressures of life—I rise because You have lifted me.

I will not live under the weight of fear, failure, or insecurity. I ascend above anxiety, above comparison, and above the chaos of the world. My place is not beneath, tossed by confusion or doubt. I am seated in heavenly places with Christ Jesus. You have given me vision, direction, and dominion.

Distraction will not detour me. I will not be pulled down by temporary trials or the noise of the enemy. My eyes are fixed, my path is ordered, and my steps are anointed. I walk in alignment with Your Word and am elevated with intention. What You have spoken over me cannot be reversed—I am above only!

Affirmation Prayer:

Lord, I declare that I am above only, established by Your hand and anchored in Your truth. I reject every distraction, every lie, and every limitation that would attempt to pull me down. Let my obedience unlock new levels of dominion. Teach me to rule with humility and serve with strength. I trust Your plan, and I rise in Your power. In Jesus' name, Amen.

Reflection Questions:

- Are there areas in your life where you have settled beneath the standard God set for you?
- What distractions must you release in order to walk fully in dominion?
- How does living above affect the way you lead, love, and serve others?

Challenge:

This week, declare over yourself every morning: "I am above only! Positioned by God for dominion." Identify one distraction that keeps pulling you away from your assignment—and replace it with a new discipline or devotion that aligns with your purpose. Journal how this changes your focus and forward motion.

Encouragement:

You are not average. You are not forgotten. You are not beneath. You have been chosen, commissioned, and crowned by the King of Glory. Rise in boldness, walk in purpose, and remember: You are positioned above only—for dominion, not distraction!

49

I AM a Kingdom Lion/Lioness – Fierce in Faith

Scripture:

Genesis 49:9-10 - "Judah is a lion's whelp: from the prey, my son, thou art gone up: he stooped down, he couched as a lion, and as an old lion; who shall rouse him up? The scepter shall not depart from Judah, nor a lawgiver from between his feet, until Shiloh come; and unto him shall the gathering of the people be."

Affirmation & Reflection

In Jesus' name, I am a Kingdom lion/lioness! Father, You have placed within me the fierce faith and spiritual authority of the Lion of Judah. I do not move aimlessly—I am led by purpose, grounded in truth, and fierce in spirit. I protect what You've given me: my calling, my family, my assignment, and my identity in Christ.

I do not cower before challenges—I confront them with unshakable confidence, knowing that Your Word is my foundation. I stand my ground, clothed in power, unmoved by fear, unmoved by the opinions of others. I am a guardian of kingdom destiny, watching, warring, and worshiping with the roar of a believer who knows their divine right.

The enemy cannot mute my voice. My roar is rooted in truth, my steps are ordered by Your Word, and my posture is one of dominion. The sceptre is in Your hand, and because I belong to You, I carry the mark of royalty and spiritual might. I move not by emotion, but by revelation. I fight not for victory, but from it.

Affirmation Prayer:

Lord, I thank You for clothing me with the boldness of a lion and anchoring me in Your Word. Make my faith fierce, my discernment sharp, and my stance unshakable. May I guard my purpose with wisdom and courage, standing firm in who You've called me to be. Let every step I take reflect the power of the One who reigns as the Lion of Judah. In Jesus' name, Amen.

Reflection Questions:

- In what areas of your life do you need to walk with greater boldness and spiritual authority?
- Are there distractions or fears trying to dull your roar or blur your assignment?
- How can you protect and guard your God-given destiny with greater intentionality?

Challenge:

This week, declare over yourself daily: *"I am a Kingdom lion/lioness—fierce in faith, anchored in truth, and assigned by God."* Write down the assignments or promises you feel led to guard and pray over them with spiritual authority.

Encouragement:

You were not created to be passive. You were born to ROAR! You are fierce in faith, unwavering in truth, and divinely assigned to protect what God has placed in your hands. Stand tall, stay alert, and move forward knowing that your roar echoes through eternity. You are a Kingdom lion/lioness—rise up and guard destiny with power and grace!

50

I AM a Divine Creative – Formed to Invent

Scripture:

"Therefore, prepare your minds for action; be self-controlled; set your hope fully on the grace to be given you when Jesus Christ is revealed."
– 1 Peter 1:13 (NIV)

Affirmation & Reflections

In Jesus' name, I am a Divine Creative – Formed to Invent, Anointed to Influence! My imagination is sanctified, and my thoughts are aligned with heaven. The Holy Spirit breathes life into my ideas, igniting divine strategies and innovative solutions that bring glory to God and impact those around me.

Because I am made in the image of the Creator, I carry the DNA of divine innovation. I create not only with my hands but with my heart, my voice, and my vision. My creativity opens doors, shifts atmospheres, and builds what heaven has already spoken.

I prepare my mind for action. I remain self-controlled, knowing that creativity requires both discipline and surrender. I silence the inner critic and step forward with boldness, trusting that what God has deposited in me is for such a time as this. I don't just imagine—I implement. I don't just dream—I develop. My creativity is my kingdom contribution.

Affirmation Prayer

Heavenly Father, I thank You for calling me to be a divine creative. You've shaped my thoughts, my talents, and my passions for purpose. I yield every gift to You, asking that You breathe fresh vision over the works of my hands.

Awaken in me the courage to act on what You've inspired. I reject fear, comparison, and perfectionism. Let my creativity carry Your fragrance and reflect Your glory. As I create, let it heal, inspire, and lead others toward You. In Jesus' name, Amen.

Reflection Questions

- What has God placed inside of me that I've been afraid to release?
- How does my creativity serve others and advance God's kingdom?
- Where do I need to step out of comfort and into creative obedience?

Challenge

This week, act on one creative idea you've been sitting on. Whether it's a design, a message, a ministry concept, or a business idea—start. Creativity is activated by movement. Declare daily: *"I am a divine creative—formed to invent, anointed to influence!"*

Encouragement

You were never meant to blend in—you were born to build, shape, and speak life through your creativity. Let God use your imagination as a vessel of influence. When you create from the Spirit, you don't just make art—you make impact. Keep building. Heaven is backing you.

51

I AM Patient with Power – Calm in Delay, Bold in Destiny

Scripture:

Ecclesiastes 7:8 – *"The end of a matter is better than its beginning, and patience is better than pride."*

Affirmation & Reflection

In Jesus' name, I am patient with power – calm in delay, bold in destiny! Father, I trust in Your perfect timing. I surrender my need for immediate answers, quick results, and instant gratification. You are working all things together for my good, and because I know this, I can rest in patience, fully aware that my waiting is not weakness—it is warfare with wisdom.

Lord, I refuse to allow frustration, anxiety, or discouragement to steal my peace. I will not be moved by delays or setbacks, because I know the end of a thing is better than its beginning. You are the Alpha and the Omega—the One who sees the full picture while I only see a glimpse. I choose to wait with expectation, knowing that what You have promised will come to pass in due season.

I reject impatience and pride that tempts me to take matters into my own hands. I won't operate in panic—I'll operate in purpose. I walk in step with Your Spirit, trusting that every delay has divine development and every waiting season is shaping me for destiny. My patience is laced with power. I stand firm, bold in my belief, calm in my process, and confident in Your promises.

Affirmation Prayer:

Father, thank You for teaching me patience. Strengthen me when waiting feels heavy. Remind me that Your timing is sovereign, and help me to lean into Your process with grace. Let my spirit stay anchored in peace and my heart steady in faith as I await the unfolding of Your perfect will. In Jesus' name, Amen.

Reflection Questions:

- In what areas of your life is God asking you to trust His timing more deeply?
- What mindset shifts can you make to see waiting as growth, not punishment?
- How can you cultivate spiritual boldness while remaining calm in delay?

Challenge:

This week, every time impatience arises, pause and speak this declaration: *"I am patient with power. I am calm in delay and bold in destiny. God's timing is shaping my purpose."* Journal one area where you're tempted to rush and write out what God might be developing in you through the wait.

Encouragement:

You are not delayed—you are being developed. Patience is the posture of those who carry kingdom authority. Stay calm, stay focused, and walk boldly into your next. You are being positioned for greater, and God's timing is preparing the stage for your destiny to shine.

52

I AM Kingdom Honorable – Cloaked in Integrity

Scripture:

1 Chronicles 4:9-10 – "Jabez was more honorable than his brothers. His mother had named him Jabez, saying, 'I gave birth to him in pain.' Jabez cried out to the God of Israel, 'Oh, that You would bless me and enlarge my territory! Let Your hand be with me, and keep me from harm so that I will be free from pain.' And God granted his request."

Affirmation & Reflection

In Jesus' name, I am honorable! Like Jabez, I am marked by integrity that sets me apart. My honor is not just in my actions but rooted deep in my relationship with God. Because I walk with honor, the Lord blesses me, enlarges my territory, and directs my steps. I am trusted by heaven and respected by the earth because I live a life that reflects His righteousness.

Honor guards my heart and my choices. I reject shortcuts, compromise, and deceit. Instead, I pursue excellence, humility, and faithfulness in every area of my life. I am confident that God's hand is upon me—protecting, guiding, and empowering me to fulfill my divine destiny.

My honorable walk unlocks favor and blessing, just as it did for Jabez. I boldly ask God to enlarge my influence and keep me from harm so

I can fully operate in the purpose He has assigned me. I am confident in God's promise to grant the desires of a heart committed to honor.

Affirmation Prayer

Father, thank You for teaching me the power of honor. Like Jabez, I desire to live a life pleasing to You—marked by integrity and faithfulness. Bless me, enlarge my territory, and keep me safe from all harm. Let Your hand be upon me, strengthening me to walk boldly in my kingdom assignment. In Jesus' name, Amen.

Reflection Questions:

- In what ways can I cultivate honor in my daily life and leadership?
- How does living honorably open doors for God's blessings and favor?
- Where do I need God's protection and enlargement in my purpose?

Challenge:

This week, identify one area where you can demonstrate greater honor—whether in your work, relationships, or spiritual walk. Speak the prayer of Jabez daily: *"Lord, bless me, enlarge my territory, and keep me from harm."* Watch how God moves on your behalf as you live honorably.

Encouragement:

Your honor is your kingdom currency. When you walk in integrity and faithfulness, you become a beacon of God's favor and blessing. Remember, God honored Jabez and He will honor you too. Stand firm in your purpose, and watch your territory expand with divine favor!

53

I AM an Anointed Warrior – Chosen, Precise, and Powerful in Purpose

Scripture:

Judges 20:16 - *"Among all these were seven hundred chosen men who were left-handed; every one could sling stones at a hair and not miss."*

Affirmation & Reflection

In Jesus' name, I am an anointed warrior! Lord, You have set me apart, empowered with divine precision and heavenly purpose. Just like the left-handed warriors of Israel—chosen and uncommon—I carry unique strengths that are destined to strike every mark You've appointed. I do not apologize for my difference, because I am divinely designed for effectiveness in the Kingdom.

Father, the gifts You've placed within me are not ordinary—they are weapons of impact and purpose. I embrace them with boldness and gratitude. I submit my skills to Your refining fire. May every gift within me be sharpened through discipline, intimacy with You, and unwavering obedience.

Even when my anointing feels overlooked or misunderstood, I know You see me. You chose me. You equipped me. I am not striving to be seen by man—I am moving to hit every target You've ordained. I walk in alignment, not just with talent, but with divine timing, accuracy, and authority.

I renounce insecurity and spiritual comparison. I rise in confidence, knowing that I am crafted by the Master Himself. With every step, I walk in precision. With every word, I build Your Kingdom. With every move, I fulfill my purpose—for Your glory alone.

Affirmation Prayer:

Heavenly Father, thank You for choosing and anointing me. Help me to walk with precision and courage in the purpose You have placed before me. Remind me that I lack nothing in You. Sharpen my discernment, develop my gifts, and let me be fearless in my function. Use me to glorify Your name and advance Your Kingdom with power and accuracy. In Jesus' name, Amen.

Reflection Questions:

- What unique strength or gift has God trusted you with that others may overlook?
- How can you sharpen your gift to increase your accuracy and effectiveness?
- What does it look like for you to operate as an "anointed warrior" in your current assignment?

Challenge:

This week, step into bold alignment with your divine assignment. Choose one area of your gifting and commit to sharpening it intentionally—study, practice, or teach it. Each morning, declare: *"I am an anointed warrior—chosen, precise, and powerful in purpose!"*

Encouragement:

You are not randomly gifted—you are strategically equipped by Heaven. What's in your hand is enough to hit the mark when it's surrendered to God. You've been trained in the Spirit for such a time as this. Keep your aim steady and your heart pure—because when you move in purpose, the enemy cannot stop your precision.

54

I AM a Willing Vessel – Surrendered, Sharpened, and Sent by God

Scripture:

2 Peter 1:21 – *"For prophecy never had its origin in the human will, but prophets, though human, spoke from God as they were carried along by the Holy Spirit."*

Affirmation & Reflection

In Jesus' name, I AM a Willing Vessel – Surrendered, Sharpened, and Sent by God! Lord, my life is not my own—I am Yours. Just as the prophets were moved not by their own will but by Your Spirit, I surrender myself completely to Your divine leading. I embrace the refining process, knowing that You are sharpening my discernment, strengthening my resolve, and preparing me for Kingdom impact.

I lay down my agenda and pick up divine assignment. I am not just available—I am *anointed* for the call. My heart is soft toward Your instruction, and my spirit is sensitive to Your prompting. I am not driven by ambition, fear, or the opinions of others. I move only by the voice and timing of the Holy Spirit.

Like a vessel in the hands of the Master Potter, I am shaped for sacred use. Whether You call me to speak, serve, or stand still—I respond with obedience and humility. I know that my effectiveness does not come from talent alone, but from being carried by You. I yield to Your rhythm and flow, trusting that in Your hands, I will always hit the mark of purpose.

Even when the assignment stretches me, I will not retreat. I've been sharpened through surrender, and I am sent with heaven's authority. I am not passive—I am empowered, led, and divinely aligned. In every moment, I am a vessel of honor, poured out for Your glory.

Affirmation Prayer:

Heavenly Father, thank You for choosing me as a vessel for Your glory. I yield my will, my voice, and my gifts to You. Shape me and sharpen me so that I may be useful in Your Kingdom. Holy Spirit, carry me beyond my natural ability. May I walk in such surrender that Your voice becomes my compass. I trust You to send me, use me, and speak through me. In Jesus' name, Amen.

Reflection Questions:

- Where in your life do you need to trust the Holy Spirit's guidance more deeply?
- What distractions or patterns do you need to release to remain surrendered?
- How can you posture yourself daily to be sharpened and sent by God?

Challenge:

This week, intentionally pause before speaking, acting, or deciding. Whisper, "Holy Spirit, lead me." Then obey without delay. Journal what changes when you choose to be *carried* rather than *controlling*.

Encouragement:

You are not ordinary—you are chosen, sharpened, and sent. Your surrender is your strength. As a willing vessel, you carry Kingdom weight, and everything God pours into you has purpose. You were made for this!

55

I AM a Disciple in Training – Taught by the Spirit

Scripture:

"As the deer pants for streams of water, so my soul pants for you, my God." — **Psalm 42:1 (NIV)**

Affirmation & Reflection

In Jesus' name, I am a disciple in training—taught by the Spirit and sent with power! Like the deer longs for water, my soul hungers to learn, to grow, and to be filled with the living wisdom that only comes from God. I do not pursue knowledge for pride or performance—but because I long to know Him more deeply.

I surrender to the teaching of the Holy Spirit, who reveals truth to my heart and writes it upon my mind. I do not depend solely on human instruction, but I lean into the guidance of the Spirit, who is my Counselor, Comforter, and Teacher. My desire to learn is rooted in my desire to walk in divine purpose.

As I study, I am strengthened. As I listen, I am led. As I obey, I am sent. I am not idle in my learning—I am being prepared for kingdom impact. Every lesson, every test, and every encounter with God is shaping me into a vessel that carries both wisdom and authority.

Affirmation Prayer

Holy Spirit, I yield myself as a student in Your classroom. Teach me, correct me, and pour into me all that I need for the journey ahead.

May my hunger for You grow daily. Let every word I read and every truth You whisper stir a deeper passion for obedience. I do not learn just to know—I learn to follow, to serve, and to glorify You. Shape me into a bold disciple, fully trained and fully sent. In Jesus' name, Amen.

Reflection Questions

- In what areas of your life are you sensing the Spirit's invitation to grow deeper?
- How can you make space for the Holy Spirit to be your primary teacher?
- Are there lessons you've been resisting that may actually be preparation for your next assignment?

Challenge

This week, carve out dedicated time to sit with the Word and ask, "Holy Spirit, what do You want to teach me today?" Journal what you sense. Look for opportunities to live out what you've learned, even in small acts of obedience.

Encouragement

You are not just learning—you are becoming. God is training you for more than survival; He is preparing you to walk in power, speak with boldness, and live on mission. Stay teachable. Stay hungry. Your classroom may be quiet now, but your commission is coming!

56

I AM Authentically Called – Unapologetically Me, Unshakably His

Scripture:

Psalm 51:17 – *"The sacrifices of God are a broken spirit; a broken and contrite heart, O God, you will not despise."*

Affirmation & Reflection

In Jesus' name, I am authentically called! I come before You, Lord, with an open heart, withholding nothing. I do not have to pretend or perform before You because You see me as I truly am. My flaws, my struggles, my victories, and my failures—You know them all, yet You love me completely.

I refuse to wear a mask or hide behind pride. Instead, I surrender my heart to You, fully and sincerely. My worship is real, my repentance is genuine, and my love for You is pure. You do not desire perfection from me—You desire truth in my innermost being. So I bring You my brokenness, my weaknesses, and my true self, knowing that You will shape me into who You've called me to be.

I am not defined by the opinions of others; I am defined by Your truth. I walk in integrity because my heart belongs to You. The world may try to change me, but I remain steadfast in my identity in Christ. I am fearfully and wonderfully made, created for Your purpose, and chosen to bring You glory.

Holy Spirit, help me to live authentically before You and before others. Let my words, my actions, and my faith reflect the real transformation You are doing in me. I will not compare myself to others or strive to be someone I'm not. I will simply be who You created me to be—a child of God, real, transparent, and fully surrendered to You.

Affirmation Prayer:

Father, I thank You that I don't have to hide who I am before You. You see my heart, and You accept me just as I am. Help me to always walk in authenticity, never striving for man's approval but seeking only Yours. Keep my heart pure, my motives sincere, and my spirit humble. Let my life be a reflection of Your grace and truth. In Jesus' name, Amen.

Reflection Questions:

- Do you feel like you can be completely honest and open with God? Why or why not?
- Are there areas in your life where you feel pressure to perform rather than be authentic?
- How can you embrace your true identity in Christ and walk in freedom?

Challenge:

This week, take a moment to examine your heart before God. Journal your thoughts, confess any areas where you've been holding back, and ask the Holy Spirit to help you live authentically. Let go of comparison, self-doubt, and the need for approval—simply be who God has called you to be!

Encouragement:

God honors a heart that is real, open, and surrendered to Him. Walk in authenticity, knowing that your true self is loved, accepted, and transformed by the Great I AM!

57

I AM Moved with Compassion – a Heart Aligned with Heaven

Scripture:

Isaiah 61:1 *- "The Spirit of the Lord GOD is upon me, because the LORD has anointed me to bring good news to the poor; He has sent me to bind up the brokenhearted, to proclaim liberty to the captives, and the opening of the prison to those who are bound."*

Affirmation & Reflection

In Jesus' name, I am moved with compassion! Lord, You have filled me with Your Spirit and aligned my heart with heaven. I do not ignore the brokenhearted, the captive, or the bound—I see them as You see them. My compassion flows from Your anointing, and I am sent to bring healing, hope, and freedom in Your name.

You have entrusted me with a divine assignment: to bind up wounds, to speak good news, and to be a vessel of liberty. I carry this calling not in my own strength, but through the compassion of Christ that dwells in me. I move with purpose because my heart beats in rhythm with Yours.

I do not run from the pain of others—I walk toward it with bold empathy. I am not hardened by the world—I remain tender, Spirit-led, and full of grace. My compassion is not passive; it activates healing. It bridges divides, lifts burdens, and ushers in the presence of God.

Holy Spirit, make me sensitive to Your promptings. Teach me to weep with those who weep and rejoice with those who rejoice. Let my words carry comfort, my prayers stir hope, and my presence reflect the nearness of Christ. I am not moved by emotion alone—I am moved by You.

Affirmation Prayer:

Father, thank You for aligning my heart with Yours. Anoint me daily to move with compassion, to see with spiritual eyes, and to love without limits. Keep me humble, willing, and ready to serve wherever You send me. Let my life be a living testimony of Your mercy and power. In Jesus' name, Amen.

Reflection Questions:

- Who in your life is waiting to experience God's compassion through you?
- How does being "moved with compassion" align with your kingdom assignment?
- In what ways can you actively reflect the love and freedom of Isaiah 61?

Challenge:

This week, be intentional about aligning your actions with God's heart. Ask the Holy Spirit to lead you to someone in need of encouragement or healing. Show up with compassion, knowing you are walking in your calling.

Encouragement:

Being moved with compassion is more than a feeling—it's a kingdom response. As your heart aligns with heaven, your life becomes a channel of healing, freedom, and good news. You are not just empathetic. You are anointed, appointed, and compassionately sent.

58

I AM a Kingdom Initiator – Bold in Faith, Ready for Assignment

Scripture:

Genesis 7:1-5 – "Then the Lord said to Noah, 'Go into the ark, you and all your household, for I have seen that you are righteous before Me in this generation... And Noah did all that the Lord had commanded him.'"

Affirmation & Reflection

In Jesus' name, I am a Kingdom Initiator! I am not waiting on a sign—I am moving in obedience. Like Noah, I am bold in faith and ready for divine instruction. I act when God speaks. I respond when Heaven sends. I move in purpose, not passivity, because I trust the voice of the One who calls me.

Lord, I thank You for positioning me in this generation to carry out Your will. Even when the assignment seems strange, uncomfortable, or unpopular, I will move with confidence and urgency. I will prepare in private so I can lead with power in public. I don't wait for perfect conditions—I obey because I believe.

I reject spiritual delay, hesitation, and fear. I am not reactive to the world—I am proactive in the Kingdom. I listen, I build, I move. I steward the instructions of God with precision and reverence. Just as Noah was entrusted with an ark that would save generations, I am entrusted with assignments that carry legacy and purpose.

Holy Spirit, train me to be sensitive to Your direction and courageous in execution. Make me a leader who builds before the rain. Let my faith inspire movement in others. I will not wait for validation—I already have Your word.

Affirmation Prayer:

Father, thank You for trusting me with purpose. Give me the discipline to prepare, the courage to move, and the faith to obey swiftly. Let me not delay what You've commanded. May my obedience be complete, my preparation be intentional, and my heart remain open to Your voice. I am bold in faith and ready for my assignment. In Jesus' name, Amen.

Reflection Questions:

- Where is God asking you to move before the storm comes?
- What does it look like to prepare in faith when no one else understands your assignment?
- Are there areas where you've been waiting for confirmation instead of obeying God's original instruction?

Challenge:

This week, take one bold step toward what God has instructed you to do—whether it's starting something new, finishing what He gave you, or preparing behind the scenes. Trust that obedience now will produce impact later.

Encouragement:

Kingdom initiators don't wait for applause—they move at the sound of God's voice. Your obedience today sets the foundation for someone else's deliverance tomorrow. Build the ark. The rain will come—but you'll already be ready.

59

I AM True to My Calling

Scripture:

Luke 1:38 – *"Behold, I am the servant of the Lord; let it be to me according to your word."*

Affirmation & Reflection

In Jesus' name, I am true to my calling!

Lord, just as Mary humbly and boldly responded to Your divine assignment, I too say, "Let it be to me according to Your word." I do not shrink back, fake strength, or hide behind fear. I move forward as a servant, anchored in Your truth and aligned with Heaven's purpose.

I do not strive to be someone else or chase after counterfeit approval. I am grounded in who You've created me to be—whole, honest, and authentically Yours. The calling on my life is not for performance but for obedience. I choose to walk in truth, even when it costs me comfort.

I embrace my identity in Christ with full assurance. I am not driven by image but by impact. I am not perfect, but I am pure in motive, open in spirit, and committed to what You've placed in my hands. I speak, serve, and lead with integrity because Your word is alive in me.

Even when others don't understand or celebrate my assignment, I remain steadfast. My authenticity is not a weakness; it is a weapon. And as I walk boldly in who I truly am, Heaven backs me up. I am true to my calling—anchored, assured, and assigned by God.

Affirmation Prayer:

Father, thank You for creating me with divine intention. I surrender my identity to You, not to please people but to fulfill purpose. Help me to walk in truth, stay rooted in Your Word, and live in alignment with Heaven's agenda for my life. Let me never compromise my calling to fit in, but be bold enough to live authentically for You. In Jesus' name, Amen.

Reflection Questions:

- What areas of your life need more alignment with God's truth?
- Are there places where you're tempted to perform instead of walking in authenticity?
- How does being true to your calling bring glory to God and strength to others?

Challenge:

This week, take a bold step toward living authentically. Whether it's setting a boundary, speaking truth in love, or walking confidently in your calling—do it without apology. Declare over yourself:

"I am not moved by pressure—I am anchored in purpose."

Encouragement:

You don't have to wear a mask to be used by God. He honors a heart that is pure, honest, and surrendered. Stay true to who He's called you to be. Your authenticity is the key to unlocking someone else's breakthrough.

60

I AM Devoted – Sincere in Love, Steadfast in Purpose

Scripture:

Genesis 29:11 – *"And it came to pass, when Jacob saw Rachel, the daughter of Laban his mother's brother, and the sheep of Laban his mother's brother, that Jacob went near, and rolled the stone from the well's mouth, and watered the flock of Laban his mother's brother."*

Genesis 29:18 – *"And Jacob loved Rachel; and said, I will serve thee seven years for Rachel, thy younger daughter."*

Affirmation & Reflection

In Jesus' name, I am devoted! My heart is sincere, my intentions are pure, and my love is steadfast. Like Jacob, I do not serve out of obligation, but out of genuine love. I act with integrity, expecting nothing in return except the joy of fulfilling the assignment God has placed on my heart.

I refuse to pursue purpose with a divided heart. I am not led by selfish ambition, comparison, or empty performance. I move in love that costs me something, because true devotion is not passive—it is consistent, enduring, and rich with meaning.

Lord, I long to serve with the kind of sincerity that is not swayed by time, hardship, or delay. My love is not shallow; it is rooted in faith, nourished by patience, and revealed in every small act of obedience.

Whether seen or unseen, I choose devotion over convenience, and integrity over image.

I don't need applause to remain committed. I am steadfast because You were first steadfast toward me. You pursued me with an everlasting love, and now I echo that pursuit in how I serve, love, and lead.

Affirmation Prayer

Heavenly Father, thank You for teaching me what true devotion looks like. Give me the grace to love without pretense and to serve with a whole heart. Let my actions speak louder than words and let my motives remain pure before You. Teach me to endure like Jacob—with joy and faith—even when the journey is long. May my life reflect unwavering love, grounded in Your truth. In Jesus' name, Amen.

Reflection Questions:

- In what areas of your life is God calling you to deeper sincerity and devotion?
- Are your motives aligned with love and integrity, or with personal gain?
- How can you model God's steadfast love to those around you today?

Challenge:

This week, commit to one intentional act of love that requires effort and patience—without expecting anything in return. Whether it's a kind gesture, a sacrificial service, or a long-overdue conversation, let it be rooted in sincere devotion.

Encouragement:

Devotion isn't measured by words—it's revealed in the quiet consistency of your actions. Your love, your patience, and your steadfastness are not in vain. God sees every step of your sincere pursuit, and He is pleased with your heart.

61

I AM Spirit-Led – Walking by Faith, Guided by Divine Truth

Scripture:

Matthew 16:17 – "Jesus replied, 'Blessed are you, Simon son of Jonah, for this was not revealed to you by flesh and blood, but by my Father in heaven.'"

Affirmation & Reflection

In Jesus' name, I am Spirit-led! My understanding and wisdom come not from human knowledge but from the divine revelation of God. I walk by faith, trusting that the Holy Spirit guides my heart, mind, and steps. Like Peter, I receive insight that surpasses the natural, revealing God's kingdom truths and purpose for my life.

I reject the limits of flesh and blood and embrace the supernatural guidance that flows from my Heavenly Father. I choose to listen carefully to the Spirit's whisper, obey His promptings, and depend on His power to lead me in every decision.

Being Spirit-led means I do not rely on my own strength or wisdom, but I seek God's counsel daily. I am confident that this divine guidance keeps me on the path of righteousness, empowers my purpose, and equips me for kingdom leadership.

Holy Spirit, teach me to discern Your voice clearly. Help me to walk humbly and boldly in Your truth, living as a beacon of light in this world. May my life reflect the wisdom and love that comes from above, bringing glory to God in all I do.

Affirmation Prayer:

Father, thank You for revealing Your truth through the Holy Spirit. Help me to be sensitive to Your leading and to walk boldly by faith, not by sight. Let Your wisdom fill my heart and mind, guiding my every step. I commit to being Spirit-led in all things, trusting that You will lead me to fulfill my divine purpose. In Jesus' name, Amen.

Reflection Questions:

- How can I better tune my heart to recognize the Holy Spirit's guidance daily?
- What areas in my life require me to surrender my own understanding to God's wisdom?
- In what ways can I walk more boldly in faith, trusting God's revelation?

Challenge:

This week, practice seeking the Holy Spirit's direction in all decisions—big and small. Before acting, pause and ask, "Is this step led by God?" Journal your experiences of following Spirit-led guidance and the peace it brings.

Encouragement:

Walking by faith and being Spirit-led is a powerful way to live your purpose. Trust that God's revelation will illuminate your path and equip you to lead with divine wisdom and power.

62

I AM a Divine Worshipper – Forever Engaged

Scripture:

John 4:24 - "God is spirit, and his worshipers must worship in the Spirit and in truth."

Affirmation & Reflection

In Jesus' name, I am a worshipper wholly devoted to God! My worship flows from a heart fully engaged with the Spirit and aligned with the truth of His Word. Worship is not just an act I perform but a lifestyle that connects me deeply with the Divine. I surrender every part of myself—mind, body, and spirit—lifting my voice and my life in praise.

As I worship, I am empowered, strengthened, and positioned to walk boldly in my God-given purpose. I recognize that true worship invites God's presence to dwell richly within me, transforming me and equipping me for kingdom leadership. I am not distracted by circumstance or opinion, for my heart is fixed on Him, and my worship is pure and sincere.

Holy Spirit, guide me to worship You in spirit and in truth. Let my worship be a sweet fragrance before God, drawing me closer to Him and opening doors for His power to move through me. I will live a life that honors God, shining as a light for others to see Your glory.

Affirmation Prayer:

Father God, thank You for calling me to be a worshipper who is forever engaged with You. Help me to worship in spirit and in truth, with a heart fully surrendered to Your will. May my praise be genuine, my love unwavering, and my life a reflection of Your glory. Fill me with Your presence that I may walk boldly in my purpose and kingdom assignment. In Jesus' name, Amen.

Reflection Questions:

- How can I cultivate worship as a lifestyle, not just an activity?
- In what ways can I invite the Holy Spirit to lead my worship more fully?
- What distractions or barriers do I need to remove to worship God in spirit and truth?

Challenge:

This week, intentionally set aside moments each day to worship God beyond words—through silence, praise, meditation on His Word, or acts of service. Seek to engage your spirit fully in worship and invite God's presence to transform your heart and purpose.

Encouragement:

Remember, worship is your powerful connection to God's Spirit and truth. As a divine worshipper, your praise moves heaven and earth, equipping you to walk boldly in purpose and lead with kingdom authority. Stay fully engaged, fully surrendered, and watch how God works through you!

63

I AM Radiantly Positive – A Beacon of Hope

Scripture:

"Finally, brothers and sisters, whatever is true, whatever is noble, whatever is right, whatever is pure, whatever is lovely, whatever is admirable—if anything is excellent or praiseworthy—think about such things." — **Philippians 4:8**

Affirmation & Reflection

In Jesus' name, I am radiantly positive! My mind and heart are fixed on what is good, pure, and uplifting. I choose to dwell on truth, beauty, and all that brings honor to God's Kingdom. I refuse to be weighed down by negativity or fear because I am empowered by the joy of the Lord that is my strength.

As a beacon of hope and light, I shine God's love into every situation I face. When challenges come, I respond with faith and praise, knowing that God is working all things for my good. My positivity is not based on circumstances but on the unchanging promises of God.

I declare that my spirit is renewed daily as I meditate on what is noble and excellent. I am a vessel of joy and encouragement to those around me, reflecting the light of Christ in a world that needs hope.

Affirmation Prayer:

Father, thank You for the gift of a positive spirit rooted in Your truth. Help me to focus on what is pure and admirable, to keep my heart and mind aligned with Your Word. Let Your joy overflow in my life and shine through me to bless others. Strengthen me to reject negativity and to walk boldly in hope and faith. In Jesus' name, Amen.

Reflection Questions:

- What thoughts am I choosing to dwell on today?
- How can I intentionally redirect negative thoughts to God's promises?
- In what ways can my positivity impact those around me?

Challenge:

This week, commit to identifying one negative thought each day and replace it with a scripture or positive truth from God's Word. Watch how your mindset and spirit begin to transform.

Encouragement:

Your radiant positivity is a powerful testimony of God's transforming grace. Keep your eyes on Jesus, the author and perfecter of your faith, and let His light shine through you!

64

I AM that Guy/Gal – Confident in My Calling

Scripture:

"I issue a decree that in every part of my kingdom people must fear and reverence the God of Daniel. For He is the living God and He endures forever; His kingdom will not be destroyed, His dominion will never end." — **Daniel 6:26 (NIV)**

Affirmation & Reflection

In Jesus' name, I am that guy/gal! I stand firm, confident in the divine calling placed on my life. I walk courageously, knowing the God I serve is the living God whose kingdom endures forever. No matter the challenges I face, I am empowered by His eternal dominion and unstoppable power. I lead with boldness and purpose because I understand that my authority is rooted in His everlasting kingdom.

I refuse to be intimidated by fear or doubt. Instead, I embrace my God-given identity, walking in faith and integrity. I am a leader, a trailblazer, and a vessel of Kingdom impact. My steps are ordered by the Lord, and I move with the confidence that comes from knowing He reigns over all.

Affirmation Prayer:

Father, thank You for calling me and equipping me to walk boldly in my purpose. Help me to be courageous in every step I take and to trust in Your everlasting kingdom. Strengthen me to lead with humility and power, always honoring You in my actions. Let my life declare Your dominion and bring glory to Your name. In Jesus' name, Amen.

Reflection Questions:

- How can I step more confidently into the calling God has given me?
- What fears or doubts do I need to surrender to God today?
- In what ways can I lead courageously in my family, community, or workplace?

Challenge:

This week, identify one bold step you can take to move closer to your kingdom assignment. Speak it aloud, pray over it, and take action with confidence, trusting that God's power goes before you.

Encouragement:

You are chosen, anointed, and equipped by the living God. Walk with confidence and courage, knowing that the Kingdom of God is eternal—and you are a vital part of His plan!

65

I AM a Fireball – Ignited by the Spirit, Unstoppable in Purpose

Scripture:

"But if I say, 'I will not mention His word or speak anymore in His name,' His word is in my heart like a fire, a fire shut up in my bones. I am weary of holding it in; indeed, I cannot." — **Jeremiah 20:9 (NIV)**

Affirmation & Reflection

In Jesus' name, I am a fireball! I am ignited by the Holy Spirit and driven by divine purpose. There is a fire in my bones that refuses to be silenced, a passion for truth that cannot be quenched. I don't shrink back. I step forward—boldly, fervently, and fearlessly—because I know who called me and why I was sent.

The world may try to dim my flame, but I burn brighter. The enemy may try to mute my voice, but I speak louder. I am not lukewarm, I am ablaze—with power, love, and a sound mind. What God has placed in me will not stay dormant. I move with urgency, live with conviction, and operate with divine clarity.

I have been touched by the altar of heaven. I am not afraid to stir things up, break chains, and call people into the light. My passion is not performance—it is purpose. My energy is not for show—it is for service. I am consumed by the mission of the kingdom, and I will not apologize for my fire.

Affirmation Prayer:

Father, thank You for setting me ablaze with Your Spirit. May I never lose my passion for Your presence or grow weary in doing Your will. Stir up every gift inside of me. Let my words carry weight, and my walk reflect Your power. I will not hold back—I will burn with holy fire and fulfill my kingdom assignment with boldness. In Jesus' name, Amen.

Reflection Questions:

- What are you passionate about that God has placed in your spirit?
- Where have you been holding back your fire, and why?
- How can you allow God to fully ignite your purpose this season?

Challenge:

This week, boldly share what God has put on your heart. Whether it's a word of encouragement, a testimony, or a step of obedience—don't hold back. Let the fire speak.

Encouragement:

You are a fireball—not by accident, but by anointing. The Spirit of God has ignited something powerful within you. Don't dim it. Let it burn, let it speak, let it move. You were born to set things ablaze for the glory of God!

Encouragement:

You are a fireball—unstoppable, unshakable, and set apart for God's glory. The world needs your light, your passion, and your voice. Let your fire burn, and never let it go out!

66

I AM Steady and Strong – Unmoved in Faith, Unshaken in Purpose

Scripture:

"And then as a widow until she was eighty-four, she never left the temple but worshiped night and day, fasting and praying." **– Luke 2:37 (NIV)**

Affirmation & Reflection

In Jesus' name, I am steady and strong—unmoved in faith, unshaken in purpose. Like the prophetess Anna, I remain faithful in the presence of the Lord. I do not waver with the winds of distraction or discouragement, but stay rooted in worship, fasting, and prayer.

My consistency is not based on feelings, but on my conviction. I am anchored in God's Word, and I show up—day and night, season after season, because He is worthy and His purpose in me is worth it. The world may be unpredictable, but I serve a God who is the same yesterday, today, and forever—and I reflect His faithfulness.

Even when I do not see immediate results, I remain diligent, for I know that obedience over time produces fruit that lasts. I am not chasing moments; I am building momentum. I walk in rhythm with the Spirit, showing up in the secret place and in public spaces with the same level of integrity.

Holy Spirit, teach me to be steadfast like Anna—consistent in devotion, consistent in character, consistent in my kingdom call. Let my daily walk become an offering of worship, marked by perseverance and powered by grace.

Affirmation Prayer:

Father, thank You for being the Rock that never shifts. Strengthen me to mirror Your faithfulness in how I live, love, and lead. Help me to keep showing up, even when no one sees, and to serve with joy and discipline. May my faithfulness bring glory to You and bear witness to the power of consistency in a world that gives up too soon. In Jesus' name, Amen.

Reflection Questions:

- Where in your life do you feel God calling you to be more consistent?
- What disciplines or habits help anchor your purpose daily?
- How can you protect your spiritual rhythm when life becomes busy or difficult?

Challenge:

This week, commit to one spiritual discipline—such as prayer, worship, or reading the Word—every day at a set time. Track your faithfulness, and journal how showing up consistently strengthens your spirit.

Encouragement:

Heaven notices what you do consistently, not just occasionally. You don't need to be loud to be powerful—just faithful. Keep showing up. Keep building. You are steady. You are strong. You are unshaken in purpose.

67

I AM Rejoicing Always – My Joy is My Strength

Scripture:

"Blessed are the people of whom this is true; blessed are the people whose God is the Lord." — **Psalm 144:15 (NIV)**

Affirmation & Reflection

In Jesus' name, I am rejoicing always! My joy is not rooted in temporary things, but in the eternal truth that I belong to the Lord. I am blessed—not because everything is perfect, but because my God is faithful, present, and powerful in all things. His presence gives me fullness of joy, and His goodness strengthens my soul.

I declare that I will not be moved by emotions or circumstances. I choose to rejoice—on good days and hard days—because my praise is not a reaction, it is my posture. My joy is not shallow or surface-level; it is anchored in grace and ignited by the Holy Spirit. It flows from knowing that I am loved, chosen, and secure in God.

I walk with a joyful heart because I walk with the Lord. I celebrate His promises, and I trust His timing. Even in waiting, I praise. Even in trials, I sing. I will not allow the world to steal my smile or silence my shout. My joy is a weapon. My joy is a witness. My joy is my strength.

Holy Spirit, help me radiate the joy of the Lord in every season. Let my life reflect Your light, and may my rejoicing bring hope to those who are weary. I live with contagious gladness because my God reigns—and that truth will forever be my reason to rejoice.

Affirmation Prayer:

Father, thank You for being the source of my joy. You bless me with more than happiness—you fill me with peace, purpose, and unshakable confidence. Teach me to rejoice always, even when I don't feel like it, because You are always worthy. Let my joy be real, powerful, and rooted in You. In Jesus' name, Amen.

Reflection Questions:

- What does rejoicing look like in your life right now?
- How can you choose joy in the middle of your current circumstances?
- Who around you needs to experience the overflow of your joy in the Lord?

Challenge:

This week, declare a *joy fast*—no complaining, no self-pity, no comparison. Instead, write down three reasons to rejoice each day. Let praise rise above problems, and let joy lead the way.

Encouragement:

You are blessed because the Lord is your God. Your joy is not fragile—it's fortified by heaven. Rejoice boldly, because your joy tells the world that your God is real, and He is good!

68

I AM Delivered – Set Free to Set Others Free

Scripture:

Moses answered the people, "Do not be afraid. Stand firm and you will see the deliverance the Lord will bring you today. The Egyptians you see today you will never see again." — **Exodus 14:13 (NIV)**

Affirmation & Reflection

In Jesus' name, I AM delivered—set free to set others free. The chains that once held me are broken. What once chased me, God has defeated. I am no longer a prisoner of fear, shame, addiction, or past mistakes. I have witnessed the hand of God move on my behalf, and today I walk in the power of that deliverance.

Like the children of Israel standing at the edge of the Red Sea, I too have faced what looked impossible. But the Lord fought for me. He stood between me and my enemies, and He opened a path forward when there was no way. I no longer look back in fear—I press forward with courage, calling others to come and see what God can do.

I don't carry the weight of yesterday because I've been set free with purpose. My freedom is not just for me—it's for the next person waiting for their breakthrough. I am a testimony of His power, a carrier of His glory, and a vessel of hope for those still bound. I walk boldly into every assignment, knowing that the same God who delivered me walks with me.

Affirmation Prayer:

Father, thank You for delivering me—body, soul, and spirit. Thank You for fighting battles I didn't know how to fight and for silencing the voices that tried to enslave me. I will not return to bondage, and I will not fear what You've already conquered. Use my freedom to draw others to You. Let my life speak of Your power, Your mercy, and Your promise to deliver. In Jesus' name, Amen.

Reflection Questions:

- What "Egyptians" has God delivered you from—old habits, people, situations, or mindsets?

- Are you still looking back at something God has already freed you from?

- How can you use your testimony to bring encouragement or deliverance to someone else?

Challenge:

This week, write down three areas where God has delivered you. Share one with someone who may be going through a similar struggle. Be intentional about speaking freedom and faith into others. Your testimony is a key that unlocks someone else's breakthrough.

Encouragement:

The enemy lost his grip on you the moment you trusted God's plan. Walk confidently in your freedom. You are no longer bound—you are chosen, redeemed, and released for kingdom purpose. You are delivered—and now you deliver others.

69

I AM Clean – Purified by Grace, Positioned for Purpose

Scripture:

"But if we walk in the light, as He is in the light, we have fellowship with one another, and the blood of Jesus, His Son, purifies us from all sin." – 1 John 1:7 (NIV)

Affirmation & Reflection

In Jesus' name, I AM Clean – purified by grace and positioned for purpose! I no longer live under the weight of guilt, shame, or sin. Through the blood of Jesus, I have been washed, renewed, and made whole. My past no longer defines me; the light of Christ now illuminates my path and calls me into fellowship with others who are also walking in truth.

I am not afraid to walk boldly because I know I have been made righteous by faith. I do not hide in darkness—I step into the light. I am a living testimony of God's redeeming power. Every scar has become a story of His grace, and every failure has become a reminder of His faithfulness.

I stand firm in my identity, clothed in purity, not of my own doing but by the work of the cross. I walk with clarity, knowing my assignment is rooted in the truth that I have been cleansed for a greater purpose. I lead with a clean heart, a clear mind, and a Spirit-filled soul.

Affirmation Prayer:

Father, thank You for cleansing me with the blood of Jesus. Thank You for calling me into the light and restoring every broken piece of my life. I receive Your grace and walk in the purity You've given me. Use me, Lord, for Your glory. Let my life reflect Your holiness and draw others into the freedom I've found in You. In Jesus' name, Amen.

Reflection Questions:

- What areas of your life do you need to surrender to fully walk in the light?
- How does knowing you've been made clean change the way you show up in your purpose?
- What steps can you take this week to walk confidently in your God-given identity?

Challenge:

This week, identify and release any guilt or shame you've been carrying. Speak the truth of your identity daily: *"I am clean, I am called, and I am covered by the blood of Jesus."* Walk in that truth and encourage someone else to do the same.

Encouragement:

Your cleansing is not temporary—it's eternal. Jesus didn't just wash you; He appointed you. So rise up, walk in your purpose, and lead with a clean heart. You are not who you were. You are clean. You are chosen. You are commissioned.

70

I AM Renewed – Restored by His Spirit, Empowered for New Beginnings

Scripture:

"Therefore we do not lose heart. Though outwardly we are wasting away, yet inwardly we are being renewed day by day." — **2 Corinthians 4:16 (NIV)**

Affirmation & Reflection

In Jesus' name, I AM Renewed! Every day, the Spirit breathes new life into my soul. Though I may face challenges or weariness on the outside, my inner man is continually restored, strengthened, and refreshed by God's unending grace.

I refuse to be defined by past failures or setbacks. Instead, I rise each day empowered with fresh purpose and unwavering hope. My spirit is alive and vibrant because God's renewing power works mightily within me.

I am transformed by His mercies—new mercies every morning. With a renewed mind and heart, I step forward boldly, ready to fulfill the kingdom assignment laid out for me. I embrace growth, I pursue spiritual maturity, and I lead with the strength God provides.

Affirmation Prayer:

Father, thank You for renewing my spirit daily. When I feel weak or discouraged, remind me that Your power is made perfect in my weakness. Restore my soul and equip me to walk confidently in the calling You have placed on my life. Fill me afresh with Your Spirit to accomplish every purpose You have ordained. In Jesus' name, Amen.

Reflection Questions:

- What areas of your life need God's renewing touch right now?
- How can you intentionally cultivate spiritual renewal daily?
- What fresh purpose is God calling you to embrace today?

Challenge:

This week, spend time each day asking God to renew your heart and mind. Journal any changes you notice in your perspective, strength, or peace. Share your testimony of renewal with someone who needs encouragement.

Encouragement:

God's power to renew is limitless. No matter what you face, His Spirit is ready to restore you and prepare you for your divine purpose. Step into your renewed identity and walk boldly as the kingdom leader God has called you to be.

71

I AM Transformed – Renewed in Spirit

Scripture:

"And we all, who with unveiled faces contemplate the Lord's glory, are being transformed into his image with ever-increasing glory, which comes from the Lord, who is the Spirit." – **2 Corinthians 3:18 (NIV)**

Affirmation & Reflection

In Jesus' name, I AM Transformed! Transformation is not optional for those who desire to walk in God's purpose – it is essential. The old ways, old mindsets, and former identities must fall away so that the new creation, empowered by the Holy Spirit, can rise and fulfill God's divine calling.

God's transformation is a divine refining process – it shapes my character, aligns my heart, and empowers my spirit to lead with integrity, humility, and power. Without transformation, I risk walking in weakness, stagnation, or distraction. But through this renewing work, I am made strong, clear-minded, and courageous – fully equipped to impact my generation for the kingdom.

Every area of my life is subject to this necessary change. I embrace God's refining fire, knowing that it purifies my motives, strengthens my faith, and expands my influence. My transformation is the foundation of my spiritual growth, the wellspring of my leadership, and the key to fulfilling my kingdom assignment.

Affirmation Prayer:

Heavenly Father, I thank You for Your relentless work of transformation in my life. I receive Your refining power that renews my mind and reshapes my heart. Help me surrender fully to Your Spirit, that I may be empowered to walk boldly in the purpose You have ordained for me. Let my life be a living testimony of Your transformative grace. In Jesus' name, Amen.

Reflection Questions:

- Why is transformation necessary for you to walk fully in God's purpose?

- How have you seen God begin to change you, and where do you still need His work?

- What old habits or beliefs do you need to release to embrace your new identity in Christ?

Challenge:

This week, commit to one intentional step toward transformation—whether through prayer, reading Scripture, or seeking accountability. Let go of what holds you back and invite God's Spirit to renew you daily. Share your journey with someone who will encourage and support you.

Encouragement:

Transformation is God's divine mandate for every believer called to leadership and purpose. It is through this necessary change that you will experience freedom, strength, and clarity to fulfill your kingdom assignment. Trust the process, lean into the Spirit's work, and watch as you are shaped into the person God created you to be.

72

I AM Sanctified

Scripture:

"Sanctify them by the truth; Your word is truth." — **John 17:17**

Affirmation & Reflection:

In Jesus' name, I am sanctified. I am set apart for God's purpose, cleansed by His truth, and made holy through His Word. I am not who I used to be—I am being transformed daily by the renewing of my mind. The world no longer defines me; the truth of God's Word shapes my identity.

Father, I thank You for sanctifying me through Your truth. Your Word is alive in me, washing away everything that does not align with Your will. I choose to walk in holiness, not by my own strength, but by the power of the Holy Spirit working in me. I surrender my heart, my thoughts, and my desires to You, knowing that Your refining process is making me more like Christ.

Lord, I declare that I will not conform to the standards of this world. I am called to be different, to be a light in the darkness, and to reflect Your glory. I welcome Your correction, Your wisdom, and Your discipline because I know that through them, I am being made into a vessel fit for Your use. I trust that as I remain in Your Word, You will continue to purify and strengthen me.

Affirmation Prayer:

Father, thank You for setting me apart for Your glory. Sanctify me daily through Your Word and purify my heart so that I may walk in righteousness. Keep me grounded in truth, and help me to reject anything that does not honor You. I declare that I am sanctified, made holy, and called for a purpose. In Jesus' name, Amen.

Reflection Questions:

- How can I allow God's Word to sanctify me in my daily life?
- Are there any areas where I need to surrender more fully to God's refining process?
- How does knowing I am sanctified change the way I see myself and my purpose?

Challenge:

Today, set aside time to meditate on **John 17:17**. Ask the Holy Spirit to reveal any areas of your life that need refining. Write down a verse from Scripture that speaks to your heart, and commit to applying it in a practical way this week.

Encouragement:

Sanctification is a process, and God is faithful to complete the work He has begun in you. You are not alone—He is guiding you, strengthening you, and making you holy through His truth. Keep pressing into His Word, and trust that you are sanctified in Jesus' name.

WRITE YOUR PERSONAL 'I AM' DECLARATIONS:

In Jesus Name, I AM

_____

_____

_____

In Jesus Name, I AM

_____

_____

_____

In Jesus Name, I AM

_____

_____

_____

In Jesus Name, I AM

_____

_____

_____

WRITE YOUR PERSONAL 'I AM' DECLARATIONS:

In Jesus Name, I AM

_____
_____
_____

In Jesus Name, I AM

_____
_____
_____

In Jesus Name, I AM

_____
_____
_____

In Jesus Name, I AM

_____
_____
_____

www.ingramcontent.com/pod-product-compliance
Lightning Source LLC
Chambersburg PA
CBHW062109080426
42734CB00012B/2807